THE
EIGHTH
KEY
TO
COLOUR

Dedicated

to

APHELIONA

THE EIGHTH KEY

TO

COLOUR

Self-Analysis and Clarification
Through Colour

by

ROLAND T. HUNT
D.D., Psy.D., Ms.D., Ph.T,
Yogacharya

author of

THE SEVEN KEYS TO COLOUR HEALING,
COMPLETE COLOUR PRESCRIPTION, etc.

L. N. FOWLER & CO. LTD.
15 NEW BRIDGE STREET,
LONDON, E.C.4.

First edition 1965
Second edition March 1970

8524 3035 3

Printed in Great Britain by
Lowe & Brydone (Printers) Ltd., London

CONTENTS

AUTHOR'S FOREWORD

THIS new book, *The Eighth Key to Colour*, rings an overtone to my earlier book *The Seven Keys to Colour Healing*. In music the seven notes of the tonic scale are resolved by the eighth which completes the octave. The culminating note echoes all that has been encompassed and simultaneously rings an overtone of the first note as it leads into a higher octave.

Similarly, *The Eighth Key to Colour* is not only a companion volume to my former book but its Alter Ego. Striking the octave it resounds the old notes and leads into the new.

During the twenty-two years that *The Seven Keys to Colour Healing* has been in print letters have streamed in from countries all over the world—from students on the threshold of Awareness, from older students of the Arcane Philosophy of Light, and from a diversity of professional men and women.

The novitiates report an opening in the inner doorway to progress in Light from study of *The Seven Keys*; the older students state they have found new lucid direction from its study; the professional workers have testified to inspiration received impelling them to new aspects of research in their chosen field of service.

An example in the latter category is Dr. Benoytosh Bhattacharyya, M.A., Ph.D., of Baroda, India, a radiesthesic pioneer in Gem Therapy. In his fascinating and instructive books on *The Science of Cosmic Ray Therapy* (published by The Good Companions, Baroda, India), Dr. Bhattacharyya constantly refers to *The Seven Keys to Colour Healing* as a source of inspiration and confirmation.

The only real merit of a work lies in its power to impel

individual application of its essential instruction whereby relayed facts may be self-realized for their verity. In the progress between truth relayed to truth realized a crystal of increasing clarity comes into being. From its heart another individual speaks from his own centre of truth.

Krishnamurti has said that "the truth cannot adequately be conveyed from one to another, it can only be progressively self-realized". However, the learning of a measure of successful conveyance on the one hand, and of active realization on the other, is cause for gratification and encouragement to new effort.

The Seven Keys to Colour Healing is now going into its tenth edition and although this is testimony of public satisfaction with this book there have been long lines of Olivers who constantly asked for more—a light helping, or another helping of Light. They have expected a Roland readily to respond, and to fill the bowl a little higher next time. This Roland is willing.

The Eighth Key to Colour is the response to that yearning. As with the former book it is an essentially practical book for the 'Do-It-Yourself student living in a Do-It-Yourself Age'. These are the days when man must go to his own well and water his own seed. In Realization one has to *earn* the truth for oneself, and the spiral of fulfilment goes through three cycles: Yearn, Learn, Earn. Really to yearn means earnest seeking, and upon finding that sought making diligent effort to apply—thus to learn and earn.

This new book is intended to give the little extra impetus to the yearner to learn and thus earn—the urge that a friend sometimes gives us when we may be inclined to rest on our oars and think we have done enough, instead of forging ahead.

These are times when man tossed on the River of Life feels the stress between the relatively placid waters of the old and the onrushing currents of the new. In the turbulent stream of the oncoming Age we think, sometimes fondly and with regret, of the old comfortable ports left behind and apprehensively of whatever port lies ahead, not realizing that the

buffeting stream itself is active opportunity—transporting us
toward unity. The old waters were strewn with gravitational
silt and debris. As man presses upstream toward his Source the
waters are clearer and anti-gravitational. Man in this New
Age must pull hard on his oars to keep afloat, to crest the
oncoming stream, lest he drift backward and founder on a
mudbank.

Man is the vessel, the stream and the mudbank at its bottom.
The mudbank is the gravitational silt in his small-self which
weighs down body, mind and soul—silt of guilt. The higher
stream is that of Spirit, a stream of Light, that can dissolve the
silt, clear his channel and stabilize the vessel.

Gratitude is the most buoyant virtue in the life-vessel of
man, and is the counter to the force of foundering gravity. In
gratitude the grave attitude toward his present condition is
resolved.

This word is formed out of two words which have ascending wings, or fins. They are as the elevating fins of a submarine
that lift the vessel from out the depths. The words are *Grand
Attitude* (the second word could also be *Altitude*), and in their
confluence man in gratitude to his Source can be lifted up and
impelled forward, lighter in heart, mind, and body into the
anti-gravitational New State of a New BEing.

ROLAND T. HUNT

INTRODUCTION

THE first new step in this book is to give the progressive student an analytical Colour-Alphabet Correspondence. By means of this correspondence he can classify the frequencies of Light or shadow that portray his personality. This is one side of the *Eighth Key*.

The other side of the key contains the combined Scales of Ray Attributes which enable the correspondence to be put to effective use. A third aspect of the Key *is* that use—the resulting method afforded for rectifying imbalance of these portrayed and analysed frequencies—the removal of the residues of gravitational silt from the colours.

Experts in charge of cherished portraits painted by Old Masters have techniques for dissolving accumulated grime and for restoration of the true colours. Man also has means for removing the grime gathered in his self-created portrait and for restoration of his true colours. Aspiring man can thus step out of the shadows and transmute old-age attitudes into the Light of New Age attitudes. Every man is a portrait of Dorian Gray. Each should cherish his portrait. The change in that portrait, degeneratively or regeneratively, is each man's own responsibility.

The two-sided *Eighth Key* of instruction is an Arcane Gift, from The High Arc of Light, that has been made available by the compassionate Watchers of struggling humanity on Earth.

The Colour-Alphabet side was given by the Illumined Authority in charge of this facet of Arcane Truth to assist the author, and the nucleus-group to which he belongs, in responding to the written enquiries of aspirants throughout the world seeking enlightenment on personal problems. The Colour-Alphabet Key does not involve or require extra-sensory-perceptions in the user. It is based in vibrational rapport inhering in the Colour-Music scale. In the years of use it has never been found to fail in accuracy of delineation.

The Seven Scales of Ray Attributes, which precede the chapters on the Seven Rays in this book have their terrestrial origins in the teachings of my revered late colleague, Ivah Bergh Whitten, who received them from her Celestial Authority. The author received them, in turn, during the first phase of his assignment to aid her, and hints of these Scales were given in the Initial Course in Colour Awareness by this teacher. The Scale of Ray Attributes in terms of Colour-Virtue response has been enlarged and verified by the Mentors directing a separate facet of instruction in which the author also has an assignment.

The student applying his Colour-Alphabet self-analysis to the Scales of Ray Attributes is enabled to view the Colour Symbols of psychological traits gathered operatively within him. Viewing these Colour Symbols in terms of brightness or shadow he has available the 3rd Aspect of the 8th Key—techniques for clarification of his characteristic colours. Further, by noting his character 'lacks' he can introduce into his psychological environment the Colour Symbols which will impel activation of dormant attributes.

Through devoted application the axis of the individual's life can be trued and steadied, and the wobble of that axis resulting from continued conflict of disruptive emotions countered. These conflicts invariably leave their sediment of silt forming a barrier between flesh and its subtler vehicles of Light. This impasse of shadow can be removed only by Light.

Man is much as a planet with a north and a south pole, having an electro-magnetic axis between them. The north pole is electrical and anti-gravitic, the south pole is magnetic and gravitational. In alignment with God's Will man's electro-magnetic axis points to The North Star (The Constant,

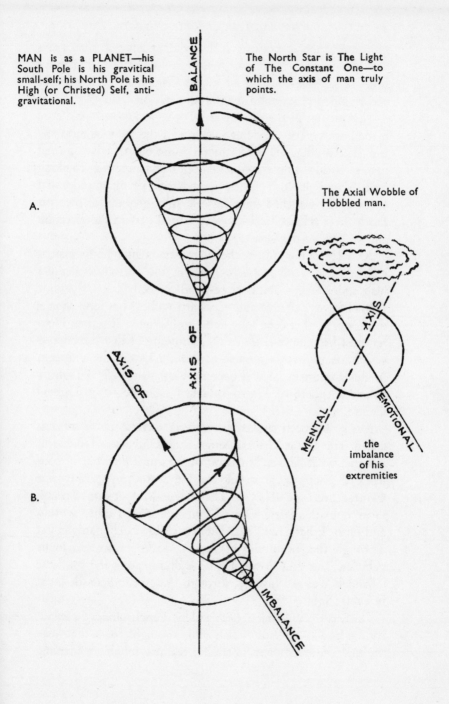

MAN is as a PLANET—his South Pole is his gravitical small-self; his North Pole is his High (or Christed) Self, antigravitational.

The North Star is The Light of The Constant One—to which the axis of man truly points.

BALANCE

AXIS OF

A.

The Axial Wobble of Hobbled man.

AXIS

MENTAL

EMOTIONAL

the imbalance of his extremities

AXIS OF

AXIS OF

B.

IMBALANCE

Christed One). In perversity of deviating self-will man's axis wobbles in the electro-magnetic astral-emotional storms of imbalance. These storms affect the firmament of his family and friends in increasing magnitudes and orbits.

This picture of the flux of Life-Forces around an axial core is the portrayal of the human cell under the sway of metabolism. The human cell is the microcosmic constructive unit of man's bodily universe—an emotionally-impelled thinking unit. Man is in turn—in the grand scale of magnitudes—an emotionally-impelled thinking cell. In aggregates of men on Earth these cells collectively play a vital part in the direction and welfare of the planetary body.

As a reasoning cell in the planetary mental body man is rightly a rationalizing server, and in this reasonableness lies his responsibility—ability to respond correctly.

Man in his perverse and wayward wobble has long sought direction. He has been long liable to his inner direction. Now he must become re-liable in the following of that direction—which means his axial alignment with the Law of the Universe. In this alignment he will become a balanced cell of Light, a balanced sphere of Light—balanced from his own Lighted Centre.

Much has been spoken in esoteric surmise upon what is called The Great Central Sun of all Universes. Unable to imagine what This is, It has remained much a matter of conjecture. There is, according to High Authority, only one Central Sun and That is The Father-Mother-Son Trinity. How does this Great Central Sun reflect into other worlds, and into Etheria and the subtler realms? The answer is: Through the infinitudes of *Atma*'s sparks encased in soulic vehicles. The Vast Power House is illuminating the Immense Chandelier of All Infinity, through the Atmic Stars of Light in every Soul.

On Earth man's coat of flesh and his densely clouded mentality are as a lampshade which dims the light from the globe within. The inhabitants of subtler realms—inhabitants having no coats of flesh, and realms knowing no night—wonder whence comes the Light that illumines these worlds?

It is The Light from The Central Sun of the Triune Godhead Which manifests as *Atma*, or the seed of Light, the true Son of God in every living Soul. It travels through an infinitely tenuous umbilical cord, or filament, of Light reaching to infinitudes at Atmic Soul-Sparks and illuminating their worlds of habitat. This is the truth in Christ's affirmation: "Ye are the Light of the World!" We illumine every world we inhabit. How many worlds do we inhabit?

The functional force inhering in the human bell, man or planet is the Directional Intelligence of Atmic Energy—God's Will and God's Energy—All-Pervasive Light. In the human cell this Directive Intelligence is the Light of the Centrosome. In the bodily universe of man It is the Divine Spark, *Atma*, in the soul's heart illuminating Its universe. In the planet It is the Directive Intelligence of the planetary ArchAngel. All work in freedom of choice within the framework of the Immutable Law of God.

Atma in man seeks to create the optimum of well-being in the human bodily universe. Its beatific plan is conditioned by the self-will of man. It is a self-will functioning with freedom of choice, in conditions of conflict, or alignment, of desires—aspiration being a higher aspect of desire, a desire infused with Soul-intent.

Rationalizing man at present exults in a mental bulge—a bulge of imbalance. He worships this bulge much as does a corpulent gourmand who cannot see the feet of his understanding. Similarly, this mental bulge obscures his inner understanding, the directive Light of Atmic Intelligence.

Man's continued tests, and rivalling contests, with Atomic fission constitute simultaneously gross ingratitude to his planet Earth, a dark blemish in the Lighted Robe of the planetary ArchAngel, and an arch blasphemy against The Creator, his Triune God. This blasphemy sullies The Light of The Central Sun, and the Light of man's own Soul.

Man attempts to blast his way into a new round of consciousness, to take the Kingdom by force. He attempts this
not only by atomic fission and jet-propulsion, but through
excitory drugs to blast through the barriers of consciousness,
and to propel him into new realms of sensory-perception.

Into the planetary body and its mental vehicle is propelled
the consciousness of man on Earth. Being also at the culmina-
tion of one great round on the upward spiral and on the
threshold of the raised-frequency of a new round, the planetary body is experiencing paralleling tests and trials to those
besetting man.

Man, without awareness of the great plan, without alignment of intent, without gratitude for the splendid opportunity
in his presence on Earth to play a vital part in that precarious
procedure, faces the grave consequences of ingratitude and the
long penance of the grave—remaining in the bonds and wind-
ing-sheets of gravity.

As man gains in knowledge and in power to release the
Energy of *Atma* within his God-Spark and within the atom—
for Atmic Energy is also Atomic Energy—he incurs equal
measure of responsibility.

The wobble of the axis of man's astral-emotional orbit in
earlier times affected only the sphere of the family or tribe,
and but to a small degree the planet of his abode. The unresolved wobble then enlarged to sway the destinies of small
nations as they became absorbed into larger nations. Now, the
unresolved wobble of man, standing in greater power, can
sway the very axis of the planet on which he lives. This
threatens the fulfilment of the role of that planet in the galaxy
to which it belongs, and the evolution of that galaxy.

This is the vast scale showing the immense measure of man's
increase of responsibility. It is the responsibility, self-incurred,
now laid upon him. It is also the ominous shadow of his
liability.

Rectification ever begins in the unit—in units aligned in
frequency of intent. Hence man, crucially alert, must quickly

c⸮ ⸮⸮ intent and stabilize his astral-emotional axis lest he wr⸮⸮ ⸮ c and annihilation of his earthly habitat, and tip the axis ⸮⸮ ⸮lanet. Such colossal upheaval would vastly delay the ou⸮⸮⸮⸮⸮⸮ ⸮g of the human-and-planetary plan.

This ⸮⸮⸮⸮⸮⸮tion to *The Eighth Key to Colour* is intended to alert acti⸮⸮⸮⸮ ⸮⸮⸮est men to crucial awareness. The remainder of the bo⸮ ⸮ analysis reinforced with remedial instruction. This preliminary is in no wise written to appall the reader or to render him befuddled with futile fears.

Its final aim is clearly to show how alert and aspiring men and women the world over can, individually and collectively, clarify their operative Colours of Service. In continuing Clarification they will learn how to gird themselves in Light, become happy warriors in the wielding of Light, and how they may enter into fuller joyous service in The Light of The Father's All-Pervasive Love.

THE MASTER COLOUR-KEY TO SELF-ANALYSIS

Indigo	Violet	Red	Orange	Yellow	Green	Blue
6 A	7 B	1 C	2 D	3 E	4 F	5 G
13 H	14 I	8 J	9 K	10 L	11 M	12 N
20 O	21 P	15 Q	16 R	17 S	18 T	19 U
27 V	28 W	22 X	23 Y	24 Z	25	26

Chapter I

THE MASTER COLOUR-KEY TO SELF-ANALYSIS

THE Christian and surnames of the individual carry the colour-symbol vibrations invoking and evoking characteristics physical, psychological and parapsychological during the formative years of the personality, i.e. progressively through the first, second and third septenary cycles of life.

The Roman Catholic Church has correctly stated: "Give me the child for the first seven years of his life, then you can do what you like with him, he cannot be changed." The second and third septenary cycles leading through puberty to adolescence serve to establish and further to confirm the native's characteristics.

If the individual is male these characteristics are developed onwards through continuing septenary cycles. If female, these characteristics are subject to modification by change of surname in marriage.

Should the marriage be the result of attraction of Soul affinities—the similarity of harmony of soulic frequencies of vibration—there is, most usually, an augmentation towards fulfilment of the individual's foundational characteristics. If marriage is impelled mainly through physical attraction, psychological conflict with the basic characteristics may result. The strength, and evolvement, of the ego are determining factors.

The consonants in the names of the individual carry masculine, positive, power. They induce action, creativity, decisiveness and will. The vowels in the names comprise the feminine fluidic spirit essence moulded and manipulated by the masculine vibrations. They are also overtones of Soul Power augmenting, or subtly guiding, the masculine vibrations.

...e of vibrations results in the traits formed in the ... child of these masculine-feminine vibrational ind... ...es.

The ... colours of the spectrum are derived from White Light. First is the primary triad of *Red* (Will), *Yellow* (Intellect), *Blue* (Faith). In the secondary colours *Orange* partakes of Red and Yellow; *Green* partakes of Blue and Yellow; *Violet* partakes of Red and Blue; and *Indigo* uniquely partakes equally of Red, Yellow and Blue.

The Chromatic (Colour) Scale in music contains twelve notes, five subtle half-tones being added to the seven of the tonic scale.

The five vowels of the alphabet (plus the spare-wheel Y) relate to these subtle musical half-tones, thus: A is attuned to A flat; O is attuned to A sharp (which is also B flat); I is attuned to B Sharp (which is also C flat); E is attuned to D sharp (which is also E flat); U is attuned to G flat (which is also F sharp); Y is attuned to D flat (which is also C sharp). As a whole, the vowels, as with the musical half-tones, constitute subtleties or refinements of distinction. They etherize, or Soul-infuse, the consonants with which they are linked. This should be borne in mind when making individual colour-analyses.[1] ..

Let us take a few examples to facilitate graphic grasp of the name and colour correspondence. We will use simply the initial of the colour to present it in our notation, i.e. R stands for Red; O for Orange, Y for Yellow, and so on. A 'drop-mark' is used to indicate vowel colours.

---

[1] The semantics of English largely derive from Sanskrit, the perfect language for phonetic correlation with the Colour-Alphabet Key. This ancient language based in cosmology was created to encompass the full range of the human vocabulary, and comprises 16 vowels and 33 consonants—totalling an alphabet of 49 letters, each with its colour vibration. That this language, conforming to the septenary law, was scientifically based upon Arcane knowledge of the Chakras is evidenced by the fact that in Yoga the sound of each letter is ascribed to a petal of each of the Lotus Centres in man, symbolizing Creative Power, or Life-Energy, flashing into the body. Thus, Sanskrit is the perfect correlative language to Colour.

First Example:

Name letters: L Y N D O N   B A I N E S   J O H N S O N

           :   :   ::   :   :   :

Colours: Y O B O I B   V I V B Y Y R I I B Y I B

Adding up the colour-vibrational units in all three names we get: *Red*—1; *Orange*—2; *Yellow*—4; *Green*—nil; *Blue*—5; *Indigo*—5; *Violet*—2.

Since this is, initially, a skeleton analysis outlining procedure we will apply but one Ray trait for each of the seven colours. (For fuller analysis consult the correspondence scales of Ray Attributes preceding the chapters on the Rays.) Thus *Red* indicates potential of Will; *Orange* indicates Constructivity; *Yellow*—Intellect; *Green*—Balance; *Blue*—Soul Mind; *Indigo*—Practical Idealism; *Violet*—Intuitiveness.

We find in the President's name the following potentials: 1 *Red* unit of Will; 2 *Orange* units of Constructivity; 4 *Yellow* units of Intellect; 5 *Blue* units of Soul Mind; 5 *Indigo* units of Practical Idealism; 2 *Violet* units of Intuitiveness.

There are no units of the *Green* of Balance. Yet, according to the degree that the 5 *Blue* units of Soul Mind infuse the 4 *Yellow* units of Intellect (producing the Blue-Green of *Turquoise*) is the measure of the President's capacity for tact, diplomacy and humour.

Taking the colour-equivalents of the vowels, including Y, into consideration we find: 1 *Orange* unit; 1 *Yellow* unit; 4 *Indigo* units, and 1 *Violet* unit. It is seen vowel-wise that the dominant *Indigo* with 4 units of Practical Idealism is lighted by accenting overtones of the Yellow of Spiritual Intellect (1), and of higher Constructivity (1).

Overall, the President's strength in Practical Idealism is supported by the power of Intellect and of Soul Mind, and the Practical Idealism is again empowered with the overtones of higher *Indigo* registration (4).

We can get a quick look at the 'punch' potentials from the initials of a name: thus, L-B-J . . . L—*Yellow*; B—*Violet*; J—

Red. Yellow of Intellect supported by the *Violet* of Intuition, with the driving force of the *Red* or Will.

Second Example: Let us estimate the potentials which impel the Soviet Premier:

Name letters: N I K I T A K H R U S H C H E V

            :   :   :   :   :

Colours: B V O V G I   O L O B Y I R I Y I

Added units: *Red*—1; *Orange*—3; *Yellow*—2; *Green*—1; *Blue*—2; *Indigo*—5; *Violet*—2.

The Premier has 1 *Red* unit of Will with 3 Constructive units of *Orange*, supported by 2 *Yellow* units of Intellect. He is strong with 5 *Indigo* units of Practical Idealism reinforced by 2 *Violet* units of Intuition, and 2 *Blue* units of Soul Mind. He has 1 unit of Balance and Humour.

Power in higher register accents his name with 2 *Violet*-frequency vowels; 1 *Indigo* vowel; 1 *Blue* vowel; 1 *Yellow* vowel.

Comparing the power units in the President's and Premier's names:—Both have 1 *Red* unit of Will, 1/1; both have the Constructivity of *Orange*, the Premier's being stronger from the incisive standpoint, 2/3, but the President having the benefit of higher vowel accentuation (1). The President is stronger in the *Yellow* of Intellect, 4/2, and each have equal vowel accentuation; the Premier has more direct Balance and Humour, 0/1; the President is much stronger in the *Blue* of Soul Mind, 5/2, but the Premier has an accent (1); both are very strong in the *Indigo* of Practical Idealism with strong vowel-accenting overtones in the President's favour (4). They equal one another in the *Violet* of Intuitiveness but with the vowel accents in favour of the Premier (2).

Intuition provides the subtlety of the oblique approach, and it can supply the surprise element in hidden motive. Such subtleties can sometimes tip the scales of strategy. *Violet* can also impel sacrifice to an Ideal.

Incidental to this comparison it is profitable to review the potentials in the initials of the late President Kennedy (J-F-K).

J—*Red*; F—*Green*; K—*Orange*. Here we see Constructive reforms pushed forward in the spirit of equity, very similar to the late President Roosevelt's fairmindedness and powerful Constructivity evidenced in F—*Green*; D—*Orange*; R—*Orange*. (And in passing we might note the late President Woodrow Wilson's two *Violet* "W"s of strong Idealism.)

It will be noted that the surnames of both the late President and the Premier begin with the initial K—*Orange*. K is a most powerful letter. Its vibration has forceful, incisive impact. As will be seen from the *Scale of Orange Ray Attributes* that this frequency impels not only Constructivity but extraversion and daring. Place the letter K on its back and it will be seen that the arms of this letter open up to a span of 180 degrees, reaching out to the horizon to dominate the world. It is a letter of expansion and of conquest—either mental or physical. The fate of the world has been touched by these two K's. It depends upon supporting motive whether this compelling vibration is constructive or destructive.

President Johnson's potentialities equip him to press forward the late President's constructive plans in Practical Idealism and to succeed with extended measures, and in new projects of his own.

Third Example: We might profitably weigh the above against the colour-vibration quotient of the British Prime Minister. Lord Home uses the name of his nativity to the capacity of highest executive of British policy and action.

Name letters:

ALEXANDER FREDERICK DOUGLAS HOME
: : :   :   : : :   : :   :   : :

Colours:

IYYRI BOYO GOYOYOVRO OI BBYIY IIGY

Summing the units: *Red*—2; *Orange*—7; *Yellow*—8; *Green* —2; *Blue*—3; *Indigo*—6; *Violet*—1.

The Prime Minister caps both the President and the Premier with 2 units of the *Red* of Will working in his favour, 2/1/1; has 7 units of the *Orange* of Constructivity, again stronger

than the other two world-leaders, 7/2/3; has a far-reaching
capacity of 8 units of the *Yellow* of Intellect, eclipsing the
President and Premier, 8/4/2. The Prime Minister has more
sense of Balance and Humour, 2/1/0; he is second to the
President with 3 *Blue* units of Soul Mind, 3/5/2; in first place
with 6 units of Practical Idealism, 6/5/5 in which all three
leaders are strong; he is second to both the President and
Premier in having 1 *Violet* unit of Intuition, 1/2/2.

His higher registration of power in the vowels is remark-
able, with 5 *Indigo* units, and 1 unit each of *Violet* and *blue* in
support. He has higher register of Practical Idealism in which
the President and Premier are also favoured, 5/4/1. The Prime
Minister also has extensive higher register of the *Yellow* of
Intellect, his 5 vowel units outleading the President and
Premier 5/1/1.

With Intellect infusing Practical Idealism on both higher and
lower levels outstandingly, the British Prime Minister has
great capacity and resourcefulness for negotiation with the
other two world-leaders toward resolving problems besetting
the planet and harassing humanity upon it. Were Britain in
equal position of power internationally the Prime Minister
might perform the miraculous, though possibly with national
sacrifice.

(In passing, the French President Charles de Gaulle has 1 *Red*
unit of Will leading 7 *Yellow* units of Intellect with no *Green*
units of Balance nor *Violet* of Intuition.)

Fourth Example: Let us take a subject known to students of
Colour. Those familiar with the writings and life's work of
my late colleague, Ivah Bergh Whitten, will find interest in
the following analysis:

Name letters: I V A H   B E R G H   W H I T T E N

Colours: V I   I I   V Y O B I   V I V G G Y B

Adding the colour units: *Violet*—4; *Indigo*—5; *Blue*—2;
Green—2; *Yellow*—2; *Orange*—1; *Red*—nil.

My revered friend functioned with 4 *Violet* units of In-tution supported by 5 *Indigo* units of practical idealism, making intuition and practical idealism dominant in her life and work, 9 units in all. She had 2 *Yellow* units of Intellect, 2 *Blue* units of Soul Mind; 2 *Green* units of Balance and Humour; 1 *Orange* unit of constructivity, and no *Red* units of Will.

However, it must be remembered that *Indigo* is composed of all the colours of the spectrum, and my friend had 5 units of *Indigo*. Moreover, *Violet* is composed of both *Red* and *Blue*. Hence this subject could draw upon *Red* resources from no less than 9 *Indigo-Violet* units.

In the higher register of vowel colour equivalents she had:—*Violet*—2 units; *Indigo*—1 unit; *Yellow*—2 units to reinforce her dominant *Indigo-Violet* functional frequencies of vibration.

Taking just the initials of her name I-B-W we get 3 *Violet* units. It is well known that this subject performed the assign-ment of her life's work on the *Violet* Ray, having entered into that frequency of expression from the *Indigo* Ray of her nativity. That she was equipped for this transfer can be seen from the analysis.

The subject's maiden name was:

Name letters: I V A H   R I C H A R D S O N

Colours: V I I I   O V R I   I O O Y I B

Adding the colour units: *Indigo*—6; *Violet*—2; *Blue*—1; *Green*—nil; *Yellow*—1; *Orange*—3; *Red*—1.

Indigo was dominant in her early years, 6 units, supported by 2 units of *Violet* and 3 *Orange* units of constructivity. Her vowel spirit essence comprised: 3 *Indigo* units and 2 *Violet* units exalting her intuition and practical idealism.

It is seen that by Ivah's marriage and the addition of *Bergh Whitten* she gained 2 units of *Violet*, 4/2, reducing her *Indigo* units, 6/5, thus inserting *Indigo/Violet* balance, 5/4, and still with 9 *Indigo-Violet* units overall. She had by marriage less constructive ability of the *Orange*, 3/1 but gained 2 missing *Green* units of Balance and Humour 2/0.

Since the author partook of Ivah Bergh Whitten's assignment it is helpful with another known subject to show, by colour-vibration name analysis, how he was sufficiently *en rapport* to assist in the practical idealism aspect of this worker's assignment.

Fifth Example:

Name letters: R O L A N D   T H O M A S   H U N T
            :   :   :   :   :
Colours: O I Y I B O   G I   I G I Y   I B B G

Adding the colour units: *Indigo*—6; *Blue*—3; *Green*—3; *Yellow*—2; *Orange*—2; *Red*—nil.

The higher register of vowel power gives: *Indigo*—4 units; *Blue*—1 unit.

The vibrational colour chord of the initials R-T-H gives: *Orange, Green, Indigo*. These colours indicate why it was also possible for the author to be called into a second and paralleling assignment in the *Indigo-Violet* expression but which has an *Orange* overtone, proving that nothing is accidental about our names.

Sixth Example: It is illuminating to reflect upon the name of the Beloved Great Exemplar of balanced Light portrayed in the name of:

Name letters: J E S U S   C H R I S T
            : :   :
Colours: R Y Y B Y   R I O V Y G

Here we see two units of the *High Red* of Divine Will (Pure Love) motivating 4 units of Divine Intellect blended into Love-Wisdom, with 1 unit each of *Orange, Green, Blue, Indigo, Violet* all in complete balance. If 1 unit each from the *Red* of Will and the *Yellow* of Intellect is taken we see all told a balance full spectrum blending into *White*, with exaltation of Will and Intellect overlighting the spectrum of *White*.

The vowel overtones of power are 1 unit each of Divine Intellect, Soul Mind, and Intuition.

The name initials J-C present two units of Divine Will (Pure Love), the manifestation of the Love-Will of God.

These examples should suffice to indicate the accuracy of the chromatic alphabet Key to self-analysis. It provides a simple and readily usable method for analysing the functional frequencies of friends who may make appeal with their health or psychological problems, thereby to aid in their resolving.

		Red	Orange	Yellow	Green
Tints		Divine LOVE-WILL Divine Grace	Constructivity (in Joy)	Divine Intellect	Balance-Pose (Self Control)
		Gratitude (graciousness)	Enthusiasm (effusiveness)	Praise (of God)	Justice (True Humility)
		Truthfulness	Joviality	Clear Logicality (ingenuity)	Sympathy (understanding)
		Compassion	Enterprise	Apprehensibility (mental grasp)	Generosity (sharing)
		Forgiveness	Extraversity	Decisiveness	Co-operation (adaptability)
		Persistence	Buoyancy (verve)	Optimism (confidence)	Critical discrimination
		Courage	Contrition of heart	Discernment (awareness)	Consciousness (caution)
Hue		Sense of Goodwill	Sense of Joy (Warm-heartedness)	Sense of Reason (Reasonableness)	Sense of Equity (Brotherliness)
		Sentimentality (self-pity)	Self-assurance	Flattery (exaggeration)	Precosity
		Obstinacy (conceit)	Exhibitionism	Sly shrewdness	Prejudice (disagreeableness)
		Resentment (ungraciousness)	Flamboyance	Deviousness (deception)	Suspicion (envy)
Shades		Passion (carnal desire)	Discouragement	Craftiness	Lack of Judgment
		Brutality (viciousness)	Joylessness	Malice (disparagement)	Callousness (indifference)
		Jealousy (remorse)	Despondency	Vindictiveness	Miserliness (non-sharing)
		Ruthlessness	Destructiveness	Deep Pessimism	Grievance (sense of injustice)

Blue	Indigo	Violet
Divine Faith (Aspiration)	Integration (At-one-ness)	Transmutation of desires
Devotion	Redemption (recollection)	Pure Idealism
Trustworthiness (reliability)	Practical Idealism	Dedication (reverence)
Serenity (stability)	Clarity of Perception	Self-Sacrifice (self-denial)
Dutifulness (service)	Articulateness (fluency)	Intuitiveness (alertness)
Resourcefulness (inventiveness)	Liberal-mindedness (tolerance)	Apperception
Tactfulness (diplomacy)	Co-ordination (analysm) .	Artistry (realization)
Sense of Beauty (symmetry)	Sense of Unity (Love, Intellect, Faith)	Sense of Power
Ambition	Intolerance	Snobbishness (superiority)
Superstition	Disorderliness (impracticality)	Self-Esteem
Tactlessness (indiscretion)	Contradiction (falsehood)	Arrogance (domination)
Distrust (unfaithfulness)	Inconsiderateness	Subtlety
Disbelief (lack of Trust)	Forgetfulness (scattered mind)	Monopolization
Dullness Apathy (lack of Spirit)	Idolatry	Fanaticism
Inertia (extreme laziness)	Separativeness (disintegration)	Treachery

Chapter II

THE MASTER COLOUR-KEY RELATED TO
THE SCALES OF RAY ATTRIBUTES

IN the foregoing chapter of explanation and examples, in the use of the Master Colour-Key, only one Ray Attribute for each Ray was selected in colour correspondence. The reason for selecting only one Attribute for each Ray was for simplification of explanation and understanding.

For instance, the one aspect of *Will* was chosen as representative of the Red Ray potentialities; *Intellect* was selected to represent the attributes of the faculty fostered by the Yellow Ray; *Soul Mind* grouped the attributes of *Faith* inculcated by the Blue Ray, and so on.

These attributes are the product of Ray impact upon consciousness. In relation to man these are the result of impact upon man's senses and their functional faculties. The faculty is the whole for the expression of the attribute.

Although the seven attributes, in each instance, are cardinal qualities evoked and expressed in each frequency of Ray consciousness, these qualities have many degrees of diversification and grossification.

If the reader will turn to the Scale of Red Ray Attributes, preceding Chapter III, it will be seen that at the zenith of the Red Ray equal status is shared by *Will* and *Love*. At that summit altitude of consciousness *Divine Will* and *Pure Love* are one and the same. In devious human consciousness we separate these glorious principles.

Down the Scale, it will be noted that concepts of these *Love-Will* Attributes (essentially One in Principle) were diminished in man as he, the Prodigal Son, over aeons of time involuted into realms of ever-lowering frequencies of Light.

With the dimming of his consciousness his expression of these Divine Principles became lowered, grossified and separated.

It is said that as the Prodigal Son became engrossified in matter he became dissipated. He dissipated only one thing—his inherent Light. As conscious contact with his High Self (which remained at-One with The Father) dimmed so did the lowered quality of expression of the cardinal principles of *Love-Will* dim and diverge in the garment of flesh consciousness.

At the exalted Height of the Red Ray the Principles of *Pure Love* and *Divine Will* are Supreme Pink Tints emblazoned with the glory of *The White Light*, the full majesty of which is beyond the capacity of man on Earth to conceive—we see but the reflection. The Prodigal Son of God, on his great adventure, departed farther and farther away from his Source. In increasing prodigality of Light the lowering frequencies of his consciousness were expressed first in lowering *tints* of Light. When the Divine Tints lost further quotient of White Light they became *hues*. Finally, in man's pervert animal consciousness the hues lost even more Light and became *shades*.

Colour is the Symbol of man's response to the frequencies of *Life-Energy*. The auric tints, hues, and shades are the characteristic responses to *Life-Energy*.

Thus, man on Earth, at the nadir or aphelion of involution with his Divine Spark of *Atma* grossly enshrouded by his earthly consciousness, acting perversely in freedom of choice, expressed the temper of his wilfulness (fiery Red) more than the temperance of the Lighted Red of Divine *Will* and Pure Selfless *Love*.

As the Prodigal long sojourned in, and finally passed through, each successive out-bound Realm of Light, he used the creative power invested in his God-Spark, *Atma*. Manipulating, with the principles of *Will* and *Love*, the One Substance, he took part in creating the kingdoms (Floral, Animal, etc.) of his next habitat, each time sacrificing a quota of his inherent Light.

The greatest sacrifice of the Sons of God eventuated when

they were obliged to take upon themselves the highest form of his animal creations on Earth. These were the lower manifestations of his expression of *Love* and *Will*.

Earth is the lowest physical plane, the lowest planet inhabited by the Prodigal. It is his reform school, or the school of his reformation from delinquency.

Gravitating into mergence with animal propensities, exulting in illusory desires, he has with perverted will and love taken part in the creation of the astral kingdom. This illusory realm is sustained by the perverted Light of the base instincts of self-love, self-concern, self-adulation, self-protection, possessiveness, gross passion and brutality. It is pervaded by the deep shades of the soul's night and benightedness. These are the shades indicated at the bottom of the Scales of Ray Attributes —the purgatory of the Soul awaiting purgation of shadow.

In the agony of engrossment, assailed by tortuous shadow, the dimmed Spark of Intelligence stirred in the soul of the Prodigal's heart. In faint recall he yearned for the Light of The Father, and of his Homeland. At this ephelion, the farthest point out, started the Prodigal's evolutionary return home . . . toward Light.

In his aeonic upward progress the developing rationalizing faculty of Intellect (Yellow) contended assertively with the instinctive grip of animal propensities (dark Red), reluctant to be dispossessed. The residual silts resulting from these age-long mental-emotional conflicts became gravitational precipitates in his garment of flesh—bondage of magnetic silt. Caught in the conflict between desires and ideas the emotional-mental axis of hobbled man has constantly wobbled. Man has long threshed in the throes of this astral vortex.

Clarification and transmutation of emotionally-impelled thinking steadies this astral-emotional wobble. Intelligence is an attribute of the Yellow Ray consciousness. When this clear Yellow blends with the pure *Love-Will* of the Red Ray, then the warm Orange of *Love-Wisdom* expands in man in wise constructivity.

Just as a three-legged stool is more stable than a precarious two, so the Pure Red of *Love-Will*, and the clear Yellow of *Intellect* should be supported by the Celestial Blue of *Soul Mind*. Here we have the pyramid of the Three Primaries. In making self-analysis the student should examine his findings for any of these Primary lacks.

Further, when the clear Yellow of *Intellect* is suffused with the serene Blue of *Soul Mind* the refreshing Green of *Balance* is cultivated. When the pure Red of *Love-Will* is infused with the Celestial Blue of *Soul Mind* the Violet of *Transmutation* becomes available. When the pure Red of *Love-Will*, and the clear Yellow of *Intellect* are jointly suffused with the Celestial Blue of *Soul Mind*, then the bright Indigo of *Recall* and of *Clarification* is born. In self-analysis the student should again take careful inventory of his make-up to become aware of secondary lacks.

The picture presented of the engrossment of the Cardinal Attributes of the Red Ray applies similarly to the engrossment of the Cardinal Qualities of all the other Rays. Essence of each Cardinal Attribute was unconsciously dissipated as man on his long involuntary journey was exhaustively prodigal and dispersive of his inherent Light. That Light has to be regained, recollected, and purified in intelligent Awareness.

For his reorientation, and re-alignment, man must seize the opportunity to analyse, clarify, balance and raise these potentials from the mire, and offer them back to his Almighty Source with added interest—a compound interest of Light. This is the inner story of The Talents, and of the Wise Virgins who trimmed their lamps of readiness. "By thy Light and by thy works shall ye be known."

One of the great mystics of our time, Krishnamurti, when asked by earnest followers what they must do to become more adequate instruments gave one piece of searching instruction.

The essence of this is that each one, alone, best knows his own vices and virtues, his prides and his prejudices. Examine each one of these traits competently, calmly, unequivocally, reacting neither with fear or favour in self-assessment. Take the impartial, detached view without activating or involving thinking processes. You will then be at the balanced fulcrum of poise and inner equilibrium, and become steadied upon the axis of your soul's intent in incarnation. Recognition of a hindering characteristic for what it is constitutes the first step toward rendering it powerless over you. To deny its existence by non-recognition is but to damp down its fires only for it to burst forth later with renewed power.

Caution against involving thinking processes in this review is because reason, impelled by self-interest, tries to justify a trait. It acts as a scorpion that bites at the heels of truth, and if allowed continuance the scorpion becomes a dragon that puts a heavy drag on the freedom-seeking consciousness. Man habitually rationalizes to justify a habit and to hang on to it. He is holding the dragon by its tail and it is a toss-up which will be vanquished.

Such moments of poised review are valuable but they are not enough. Recognition stirs the dark traits that feed upon our Soul's Light. Recognition beckons the lurking enemy-traits from their hidden lairs out into the open. Our virtuous attributes welcome this review in Light. But our darker traits rebel in fury lest they be dispossessed of their habitat. Thus brought to Light, and held in Light, these dark propensities thresh around in our magnetic field awaiting the chance to retire back into their human caves.

These silted dark traits are the vehicles for obsessing entities —the dark traits are our traitors. The preying obsessing entities are 'the thieves and robbers' of our Soul's Light, and who would deviate us from our Soul's Intent.

In the strategy of this review the dark traits cannot be allowed openly to remain in our magnetic field there to gather more of their own kind. Practical measures must be taken at once to clarify each dark trait which is but a perversion of an attribute of a cardinal quality. The trait must be transmuted into the Attribute of Light.

The Master Colour-Key helps us in quiet self-analysis. The Scales of Ray Attributes further help us to place our recognized traits on the scales of adherence to, or divergence from, the cardinal qualities.

As we study each Scale of Ray Attributes we shall witness the position and potential of our traits. We shall become aware of our lacks in certain qualities necessary for the rounding out of our characters. We shall look for the wherewithal to bring our characters into balance.

In the penultimate chapter is polished the *Eighth Key* which will enable us to clarify the balanced attributes—with necessary techniques to raise them into the Cardinals of Light.

This is Transmutation.

First . . .
Stood forth the Mighty Archangel of the Ray of
Ruby Red. He embodied the principle of Will.
This is the First Principle of the Creative Impulse.

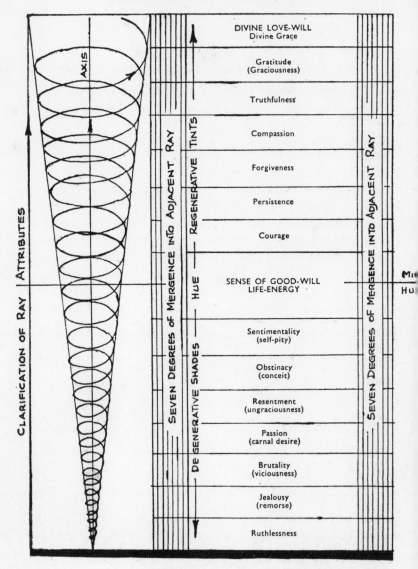

PRIMARY RED RAY ATTRIBUTES

Anti-Gravitational LIGHT——of The High (GOD) Self

DIVINE LOVE-WILL
Divine Grace

Gratitude
(Graciousness)

Truthfulness

Compassion

Forgiveness

Persistence

Courage

SENSE OF GOOD-WILL
LIFE-ENERGY

Sentimentality
(self-pity)

Obstinacy
(conceit)

Resentment
(ungraciousness)

Passion
(carnal desire)

Brutality
(viciousness)

Jealousy
(remorse)

Ruthlessness

AXIS

CLARIFICATION OF RAY ATTRIBUTES

SEVEN DEGREES OF MERGENCE INTO ADJACENT RAY

REGENERATIVE TINTS

HUE

DE GENERATIVE SHADES

SEVEN DEGREES OF MERGENCE INTO ADJACENT RAY

Mi
Hu

Gravitational silt, produced by small-self

Chapter III

ANALYSIS OF THE PRIMARY RED RAY ATTRIBUTES

THE infinite diversity of human traits and characteristics is most striking when viewing the panorama of Ray Attributes. The work of searching, evaluating, classifying and enumerating these attributes was a thrilling detective and deductive experience. And in use of the word 'thrilling' both the cheering and the chilling aspects of that sensation were involved—in consideration of the virtues on the one hand, and the vices on the other.

In his zeal, the author had carefully evaluated forty-seven attributes to each of the Seven Ray Scales. This comprised altogether over three hundred and forty attributes. When presenting these Scales for verification by the beloved Elder Brother overseeing this assignment, the verdict was given that so many vice-virtues per Ray might overwhelm and discourage the earnest student and applicant. One can have too much of a good thing. "You have said this is a Do-It-Yourself book. All right, let the student do some of it!"

The follow-up suggestion was that the lists be pruned down to seven attributes per Ray and to allow the student to fill in the gaps. The pruning and the weighing of selections down to seven proved more difficult than the probing out and appraising the forty-seven. On the thorns of choice, the skeleton scale in each case, looked like trees robbed of their flourishing leaves. Finally, it was permitted that seven virtues of tints, seven vices of shades, and one balancing overall virtue of hue, adorn the Ray Scale of each tree. This is not mere simile, for each Scale is a tree of life and growth. But the seed and root of the Cardinal Attribute abides in the Heights, whereas the tree of life in man has its prodigal Atmic seed of Light lodged in Earth, and unfolds to the Heights.

Despite the pruning of the Scales plenty of room is left for the diligent 'Do-It-Yourself' student to fill in some minutes between the degrees on each Scale. This analytical, evaluating effort can contribute to his own discrimination and advancement in understanding.

It should be borne in mind that all virtues spanning the Seven Rays have a common denominator of *Light-Love-Life*, whereas all the vices of the Rays, in pervert brotherhood, have a common denominator of neutralizing *Grey*—of devitalizing fear, frustration, and finality of death.

As the student's eye scans each scale of Ray Attributes his attention may be arrested questioningly that a particular potentiality, or propensity has been placed on a particular Ray, and contrary to customary classification and association. As a case in point, it may come as a surprise to see the vice of Jealousy placed on the Red Ray. The 'Green-eyed monster' is commonly classed with Green or Yellow.

Jealousy, it appears, is borne of insecurity and fear of loss. It is the child of self-derogation and thus in on the Red Ray. In each such case, often when the author himself has questioned the placement priorly, careful extended analysis has been given to elucidate and justify the correct classification.

The investigation, the deductions, the following of trails of traits to their origins has been akin to the eager pursuit, suspense and solving of a great mystery story. It is the greatest detective story ever written.

That story has been written by every man, within every man, on his Soul's records in terms of Light and shadow. It can be read with conviction only by man himself, the individual, under the Light of his inner Intelligence, his Inner Sun, the Light of the Son-ship with The Father from Whom he inherits his *All*.

This book has seven Ray chapters of reference. Let us then first follow the blazing trail of the virtues of the Red Ray from The Heights as portrayed in the consciousness of All the Prodigals outward bound from their Homeland in the Heights.

On the First Round out the Sons of God functioned on Realms of Soul in Soul Bodies of glorious Light and splendour. Their Guardians became the Great Archangels—Those Who returned to The Father in the First Phase of the First Round outward, responding undeviatingly to The Father's *Love* and *Will.*

Although we commonly ascribe Seven Archangels to the Seven Rays there are in truth Seven Archangels to *each* Ray of Manifestation—Three Primaries abiding in Supernal Light and Four Secondaries volunteering to play sacrificial roles in Luciferian intent. These are the Arch Forces, positive and negative of each Ray, aligned to *God-Will* and self-will respectively, anti-gravitic and gravitic, working as the rhythmic and contending tides of the mighty ocean.

(This simplification of the Archangelic System is for the purpose of explaining the relationship of The Lighted and Luciferian Archangels, respectively, to the characteristic reflection of Light and Shadow in man. In truth, multitudes of the Sons of God, as Archangels returned Home at the outset of the First Round, not Twenty-one.)

The Three Archangels in Supernal Light work directly with the Power of The Almighty in virtuosity, and the Four Who volunteered in Luciferian service work indirectly with the desire element in man's small-self consciousness. All serve that man may be tested, tried and trued—that his inherent powers may be reclaimed and his character clarified by conscious effort.

In his redemption—through his own effort—man redeems not himself alone, but collectively, mankind progressively redeems the Four Archangels from Luciferian service. That is the scope of Redemption, and the measure of man's obligation.

To clarify this picture of the Twin-Forces reflected in the Scales of Ray Attributes, One more qualified now speaks:

"The Seven Mighty Archangels of Creation are constituted, each One, of Seven aspects of the Principle exemplified. Hence we say there are seven aspects of *Will*, seven aspects of *Wisdom*, seven of *Aspiration,* and so forth.

c

"God's Gift to His Sons was the gift of freedom of choice, or as man says, free-will. For in order to venture forth into the Fields of Experience it was necessary that a motive, or incentive, be established within the heart. We call this motive 'desire'—emotive impulse. Here was the division of Truth—from Simplicity into Complexity.

"*Atma*, being a portion of God, would of necessity be in such harmonious accord with His Will and Intent that *Atma* would automatically and unquestioningly function in the Will of His Father. Therefore God did instigate a slight imbalance. This slight imbalance is in nature of de-magnetization. For God, being *Love*, is The Divine Magnet, calling His own back to Him. This de-magnetization is freedom of choice, or free-will, as opposed to the Will and Law of God.

"God's Sons were to be tested in regard to their gift of free-will, and in accord with the results of this testing would be their experiences.

"On the Ray of God's Will the first Mighty Archangel is Christ. The opposing aspect of this Principle we name Lucifer, who volunteered as Tester during man's wilful adventure. Christ chose the part of Redeemer.

"In Holy Writ it is said, and with verity, that in an instant Lucifer was cast into 'outer darkness'. For upon God's acceptance of Lucifer's sacrifice, and upon His acceptance of Christ's role, the Mighty Plan of God for His Sons was in reality consummated—the Beginning and the End, the Alpha and Omega.

"The Plan of God is inclusive, necessarily, of all Seven Principles of Creation. Thus the remaining Six Principles played, each in His particular way, those roles assumed by Christ and Lucifer, and the Principles intervening[1] did also.

"Hence, from the Golden Ray of Divine Wisdom, a Mighty Archangel of this Ray volunteered as Tester to exemplify small-self intellect as opposed to Divine Wisdom. From the Ray of Blue Transcendent an Archangel volunteered for the

[1] Note 'intervening' degrees of mergence on Scales of Ray Attributes.

role of small-self ambition as opposed to Spiritual self-less Aspiration. And so it was, and is, with the remaining Arch-angelic Principles.[1]

"In the beginning, at the Dawn of Creation, it is said that 'The Sons of God shouted for joy'. This is truth. For upon being sent forth from God's Bosom His Sons issued as a Song of Joy.

"This was their song of gratitude—gratitude for life eternal. It was on this Song of Joy that they winged forth into the Fields of Infinity. Joy and Gratitude are One, as Love and Will are One; and Gratitude is Love of God."[1]

The ineffable Crimson tones of the Principle of God's Love and Will sing out through blazing White Light in highest tints of Transcendent Pink. It is the Expression of Divine Life-Energy and of All Healing. It is the Divine Grace, that is the vast bounty Blessing All Creation.

It is That alive in the hearts of the Sons of God Whose eyes are too pure to behold iniquity, or inequity, for the two are the same. This equity is the quality of compassion—that passion that is 'with' com-passion (Salmon Pink).

The equality of Compassion is related to the balance of Truth, and the attribute of Truthfulness in the Sons of God (White infused Pure Red).

In study of the Colour Key it will have been noted that the letter 'T' (which vibrates to Green) represents the Scales of Justice. The form of this letter is balanced in its design and looks as a pair of inverted scales.

When the 'T' of balance is removed, by the imbalancing impulse of man's self-will the Scales of Truth are emptied of their ruthfulness by man's ruthlessness.

If we scan the Scale of Red Ray Attributes we find ruthless-ness at the deeply shadowed base opposed to Truthfulness at the Heights.

Ruthlessness is the result of the lack of Gratitude. Almost all

[1] Ex Master Monographs issued by *AMICA*, Temple of Radiance, Inc. P.O. Box 173, Santa Barbara, California.

of the essence of White Light has been dispersed leaving darkest Red of ingratitude—which is gravity.

Persistence and Courage are manifested qualities of the Life-Force of *Love-Will*. Persistence, on the physical level, is the scarlet hue of the clear arterial bloodstream sustaining the cells of the coat of flesh.

The clear scarlet blood issuing from the heart—the abode of *Atma*, The God-Spark—on its prodigal journey into the realms of the physical body dispensing of its Light, gathers unto itself silt and in the shades of maroon-dark-Red returns through the venous system for redemption and purgation by the Breath of God in the lungs, and the Divine Spark in the heart.

Purgation of the dark Red shades of Brutality, Carnal Desire, and Resentment is hindered by man's sense of guilt which weights the Soul's heart and beclouds its Intent. The sense of guilt (a Red Ray cloud) obstructs the purgation of forgiving of oneself.

Forgiveness should be spelt 'fore-giveness', a before-gift, a sheer gift to oneself *before*hand to shear the shackles of consciousness of guilt which weigh down the Soul. For man must fore-give himself before he can forgive others. Forgiveness thus is a gift to his Soul—a Divinely bestowed gift of Light to purge the dark cloud obscuring his inner Truth.

Obstinate in self-conceit, wallowing in sentimentality of self-pity, man is blind to the Lighted Power of this gift of self-forgiveness. Whilst his ego is enshrouded with the binding-cloths of small-self it cannot rise into the Lighted Robes of the Red Ray aspects of his High Self consciousness.

The Goddess of Justice is oft depicted blindfolded. This is symbolic of the blinding of man's conscience by lack of forgiveness and compassion. Conscience means 'knowing with'— with unmasked Truth.

All God's Creation is the recipient of God's All-Pervasive Grace. When man responds in full awareness and gratitude for the Gift of God's Grace (an aspect of Red Ray *Love-Will*), then comes the down-pouring, and down-powering, of *Life-Energy*, which is the essence of All Healing. Being aware of God's Grace is to be suffused with True Graciousness.

Man's ego facing upward, bathed in the Light of his High Self consciousness, becoming increasingly aware of the bounty of God's Love, Compassion and Forgiveness, finds his heart spontaneously swelling in Gratitude.

And in the Joy of Gratitude his heart sings and blends with the great chorus of Joyous Song that lifts All creation returning to The Source.

The Office of the Mighty Archangel of the Ray of Gold, or Yellow, is Intellect—Conscious use of Mind.

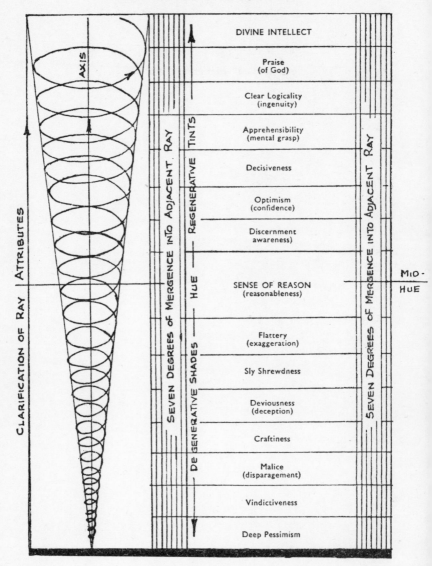

PRIMARY YELLOW RAY ATTRIBUTES

Anti-Gravitational LIGHT——of High (GOD) Self

DIVINE INTELLECT

Praise
(of God)

Clear Logicality
(ingenuity)

Apprehensibility
(mental grasp)

Decisiveness

Optimism
(confidence)

Discernment
awareness)

SENSE OF REASON
(reasonableness)

Flattery
(exaggeration)

Sly Shrewdness

Deviousness
(deception)

Craftiness

Malice
(disparagement)

Vindictiveness

Deep Pessimism

CLARIFICATION OF RAY ATTRIBUTES

AXIS

SEVEN DEGREES OF MERGENCE INTO ADJACENT RAY

REGENERATIVE TINTS

HUE

DEGENERATIVE SHADES

SEVEN DEGREES OF MERGENCE INTO ADJACENT RAY

MID-HUE

Gravitational silt, precipitated by small-self

Chapter IV

SCALE OF ATTRIBUTES OF THE SECOND PRIMARY: THE YELLOW RAY OF INTELLECT

THE Second of the Three Primary Rays of Creation is our logical next consideration, instead of selecting Orange which is the next in Rainbow sequence. It is only by our study and grasp of the fundamental potentials of the Primary Triad of the Red, Yellow and Blue Rays that the function and attributive relationship of the Secondary four Rays, the Orange, Green, Indigo and Violet, can be clearly understood. Since the Secondary Rays originate in, and from blending of, the Primaries they partake in certain measures of the Primary Principles involved.

Comprehension of the properties of this Ray of Intellect is perhaps of paramount importance to man at this time, of all times. For it is through man's perverse application of Intellect that he has produced his present mental bulge of imbalance, tipping his axis to degrees of crucial extremity. We see today the awesome creations of man's intellect threatening the destruction of mankind and the planet on which he sojourns— the plight of a planet which, verily, subsists on the Light of Souls on Earth, far more than man substantively upon it.

"In the beginning Souls created in remembrance, and intuitionally, of their Homeland, the Heights. With the diminution of their Light and dimning of their memories, their creations became less of validity and beauty.

"As Souls ventured ever and ever 'outwards' away from Home, their experiences became more sorrowful and agonising. They began to feel the necessity of developing some other faculty. This was but a vague urge born of uneasiness. This urge emanated from *Atma*, Who is ever linked with the High

Self Intelligence of the Soul. Impelled by this urge Souls began to develop a power of reasoning, or intellect, and this mainly through the medium of their 'senses'. This faculty could be fostered and developed only, it seemed, through experiences so agonizing that they would shatter, or cut through, the adamantine insulation of darkness which had formed around the Soul, and that Soul's own subtle and material vehicles.

"In God's Love and Wisdom the time arrives in the Soul's journey where man is compelled to pause upon his self-willed course and admit of the need of love and wisdom. This usually confronts the Soul upon the lowest allowable plane of consciousness. From the very depths of his own self-created 'hell' will the hardy rebel lift his eyes and heart to God."[1]

And as the eyes of mind and heart lift to God man yearns to know the meaning of the Light, the Life, the Love that inwardly bless his world. Colour is a symbol to the Soul, recalling an experience of the Soul, tuning-in to a frequency of consciousness and of memory. Colour is a symbol of *Love*— Light, Life, Love. It will be noted that each of these words begins with an 'L' denoting the Gold of Intelligence.

Love is consciousness; Life is consciousness; Light is consciousness. A photon of Light is a tiny element(al) of consciousness. There is no consciousness without Intelligence. Just as *Will* is the Father aspect of *Love*, so is *Intelligence* the Mother aspect of Energy—the Goddess of Wisdom impelling right use of Energy.

The Greeks worshipped the Goddess of Wisdom in early days as Minerva, or Pallas Athene, and in the latter days as Saint Sophia—thus man sanctified Intelligence. She was the feminine aspect of Zeus the God of Will. Indeed, the Greeks made gods of all human propensities, the traits good and bad in man, deified. An inverse and somewhat perverse arrangement, but at least inclusive.

Man in present days worships Intellect almost exclusively.

[1] Ex Master Monograph issued by *AMICA*, Temple of Radiance, Inc.

With his mental bulge, in egoic pride, he worships this faculty within himself as self-originating and self-developed. To him it is his one guide and god, rather than a gift endowed by God and an attribute of the Divine.

In this attitude is seen the immensity of the measure of man's loss of Light, the dimness of the memory of his Source. Intellect is portrayed performing precosely in perversity instead of Intellect properly appraised and applied in university; Intellect precarious in imbalance instead of Intellect poised in true balance. In the Scales of Intellect there is righteous use of Energy and unrighteous use of Energy.

In speaking of 'wrong' use and 'bad' use of Energy it will be noted that both these words begin with a Violet-attuned letter, indicating perverse use of intuition—without the complementing Gold of Wisdom.

The Crown Chakra, which looks as a radiant flower oft called the Thousand-petalled Lotus, has luminous tourmaline (Pink suffused with Violet) and a centre of blazing Gold. It depicts, in truth, Intuition guiding Divine Intellect.

Man, with his Intellect so crowned, in the nobility of his full stature offers his Praise to God. Praise, in all its aspects, rightly belongs of God, and to God alone.

The golden frequencies of Yellow symbolize and impel the discernment we call 'Awareness'. Awareness is the grasp of the fingers of mentality in apprehension. Also, it is only by knowing in the light of clear logic and reason that man can appraise. Out of the revelation of true appraisal springs the fount of high praise. The offering of Praise to God is man's response for the ability to appraise through Intellect.

Knowledge based in the Gold of Wisdom breeds confidence, optimism, decisiveness. Whereas knowledge without Wisdom—put to devious and pervert self-interests—hence without the Mother aspect of Love, results in the muddied Yellows of deep pessimism and indecision.

In true appraisal man gains exactitude whereas in flattery man falls into exaggeration. Again, in considering man's mental-emotional wobble, on the scales of balance we have on one side clear mental appraisal, and on the other side man's emotional reprisal—the emotional perversion of Intellect.

When the wings of Wisdom no longer hover to impel ingenuity in the true craftsman we have the craftiness of the fey-genius which seeks to undo and out-do.

In true discernment and awareness man can compare, in malice and disparagement he dis-pares in despair.

In wise apprehension the wheels of his mental vehicle revolve carrying intellect forward. In the vicious grip of vindictiveness he uses his apprehensive tools for mental machinations. As a wrecker of Divine machinery he becomes reprehensible.

All vicious perversions of the Golden tints of Intellect, in loss of Light become devitalized dirty shades of repulsive yellows. The dark small-self shadows benighting Intellect precipitate toxic silt which binds man's body and mires his mentality in the nether-realms of earth.

The characteristic of sly shrewdness, though by no means virtuous, has shrewdness suffused with shafts of sly Yellow light of ingenuity.

If the entangling web of shrewd small-self interests could be dissolved in the Light of service to High Self intents, the clear Yellow of Perspicacity could result.

Viewing the Yellow Ray Scale of Attributes at its centre of balance is seen the true hue of Yellow. It lies between the descending shades of mental degeneration and the ascending tints of mental regeneration. This is the fulcrum of reasonableness.

In the true spirit of reasonableness man is aided toward resolving his darkly sedimented extremities. Lifted in the pale Yellow of pure logical discernment complexity can be resolved into simplicity. In purity of appraisal man can perceive the grandeur of the most precious gift of Intellect—the jewelled instrument of Light that can pierce the clouds of unknowing, and with Lighted understanding reach up to the Heights.

Not without reason did the Greeks deify a masculine aspect of Wisdom as Hermes with his Staff of Light, and with wings upon the feet of understanding. Intellect was also symbolized by the Greeks in its twin aspects, astrologically, as Castor and Pollux—the heavenly twins.

When the two wings of Pallas Athene, Goddess of Wisdom, hover over the ego of the small-self will be hatched by the warming Light of Wisdom and flutteringly emerge, the Divine fledgling.

Then Intellect in man instead of floundering will be raised on two wings of balanced Light and be enabled to soar to the Heights of Attainment.

The Office of the Mighty Archangel of the Ray of Blue is the Bringing Forth of Soul Intent.

PRIMARY BLUE RAY ATTRIBUTES

Anti-Gravitational LIGHT——Purity of High (GOD) Self

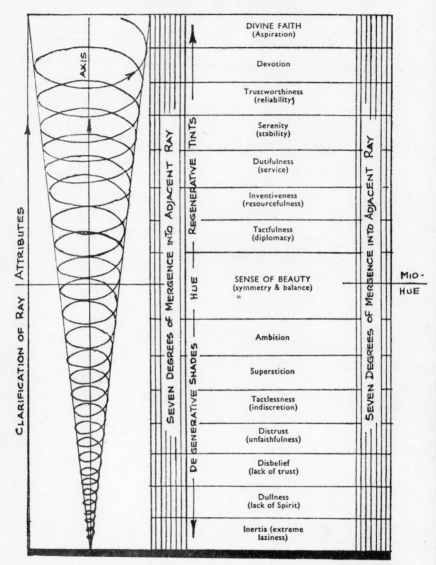

DIVINE FAITH
(Aspiration)

Devotion

Trustworthiness
(reliability)

Serenity
(stability)

Dutifulness
(service)

Inventiveness
(resourcefulness)

Tactfulness
(diplomacy)

SENSE OF BEAUTY
(symmetry & balance)

Ambition

Superstition

Tactlessness
(indiscretion)

Distrust
(unfaithfulness)

Disbelief
(lack of trust)

Dullness
(lack of Spirit)

Inertia (extreme
laziness)

CLARIFICATION OF RAY ATTRIBUTES

AXIS

SEVEN DEGREES OF MERGENCE INTO ADJACENT RAY

REGENERATIVE TINTS

HUE

DE GENERATIVE SHADES

SEVEN DEGREES OF MERGENCE INTO ADJACENT RAY

MID-HUE

Gravitational silt precipitated by small-self

Chapter V

THE SCALE OF ATTRIBUTES OF THE THIRD PRIMARY:
THE BLUE RAY OF FAITH

CLEAR, true Blue as seen through the prism, is a colour of Spirit Realms. As such it carries a slight Cosmic moisture—a crystalline dew of higher realms, refreshing and renewing to the subtler vehicles. Understandably therefore, Blue in its soothing softer tones induces Meditation.

Aspiration is the attribute impelled from the Heights of the Blue Ray, the Third Primary. Aspiration ascends in the magnetic attraction of the Principle of Faith—it is the wielder of the Substance of Faith, the moulder of manifestation.

The office of the Mighty Archangel of the Blue Ray is the bringing forth of Soul Intent recorded in the Akaska of the Soul Mind. Thus, Aspiration is the high desire to know, and to fulfil, the Soul's Intent and purpose of incarnation. It is the gift born of Will and Intellect in *Love*.

> "In lambent depths of this, our Gift,
> Is hidden deep the power to lift in tone
> The flesh of those who ask, in Faith, of Thee
> Surcease of pain and sorrow's agony."
>
> Apheliona

Aspiration is not sustained through knowledge of its parents *Love-Will* and *Divine Intellect*, but in Trust. It is not vitalized by hope, for hope is an anaemic, shadowed, word enshrouded with the winding-cloths of doubt and impaled by disbelief. Whereas 'Trust' is pure confidence of inevitability. Even the word which is its symbol is balanced with a 'T' at each end. Trust is balanced in its going forth and assured in its completion. Trust has a thrust that wields the Substance of Faith into operation—making the 'impossible' possible.

Faith has clear unobstructed conductivity. When the sick man in perfect trust touched the hem of the garment of Christ Jesus, He, aware that His Light had been tapped, said: "Go, thy Faith hath made thee whole!"

Man has been long liable to the Light of Faith. With trust he becomes trustworthy and reliable in the use of its Substance. In the balance of Trust he is bathed in the serene blue waters of his Soul Mind which refresh and inspire his physical mentality as a balm to his Intellect.

In the country districts of England where housewives still bake their own bread the term 'balm' is used for 'yeast'. Trust is as a balm to the heavy dough of the physical mentality. It is as the germ of yeast that raises and expands Intellect producing the leavened loaf—the work and Substance of Faith.

The Soul Mind serves the Intellect by its infusion therewith. This is its duty to Intellect. Both man's high sense of duty, and his conceptions and capacities for service, are impelled by his Soul Mind. Through the power of these symbols man has exemplified the attributes of Blue in the uniforms of senior civilian and national service. Man puts his trust in these.

In the spirit of devotion man robes the Mother of Conception in Madonna Blue. When the turbulent waters of man's physical mentality are stilled by the tranquillizing touch of the Soul Mind, the voice of the Spirit speaks, announcing the birth of a new concept.

Scientists, physicists and inventors conceive new ideas and utilitarian devices when intellect is germinated by the Blue of the Soul Mind. Oft when striving intellect reaches the circumference of its sphere of operation it recoils from this barrier. In succeeding moments of passivity, with intellect at rest, the Blue of the Soul Mind is able to seep through to reinforce and expand intellect, and a new idea is successfully conceived and received. Working with the Substance of Faith the new idea is shaped into manifestation.

Statesmen put to service a related aspect of this quality of the Blue Ray in diplomacy. It has oft been said that 'the pen is mightier than the sword'. The carefully chosen, quietly spoken, word has often been mightier than pen or sword. Used at the right moment it has been known to avert wars. This attribute of Blue is sometimes known as 'tact', a peculiar word for it means 'touch'. American politicians are inclined to think that European statesmen have the art of the 'soft touch'.

Tact is most inclined to function when the fingers of the Soul Mind gently touch intellect quietly inspiring a new way around a problematic obstacle unassailable and unresolvable on the level of its creation. In the turquoise of tact the Blue of Soul finds action and equity in partaking a little of Green. This results in luminous turquoise—accomplishment with the minimum effort.

There is an awakening of a certain sense of beauty in the symmetrical rounding-off of thorny problems, and obtuse (and often acute) situations through tact.

The sense of beauty—the mathematical beauty of form, figures and formulas—is an attribute fostered by the Blue Ray of Soul Power, for the Soul Mind reaches into the Pattern World where exist the forms and formulas of Perfect Ideas. Reaching in aspiration into the frequencies of the Soul Realms of Blue, artists, chemists, inventors and technicians, have been enabled to bring through concepts of beauty, and simplification of operation, in subjects they are endeavouring to objectify.

On the descending scale of attributes below the hue, in ever deepening shades, are the dark counterparts of Aspiration—selfish ambition; Devotion becomes superstition; Faith—faithlessness; Trust—distrust. Serenity becomes dullness and apathetic lack of Spirit; tact turns to indiscretion; confidence of beauty is transformed to the ugliness of fearful uncertainty. Service robbed of its dignity takes on the vileness of servility, and the forward moving wheels of initiative are stilled into inertia. The confident steps of Belief founder in the infidelity of disbelief, and the Word of Faith is overcome by the deluge of many words.

These are the steps up and down the ladder of the Blue Scale of Attributes and propensities. It should be remembered that the original forty-nine steps to this ladder have been, for purpose of simplification, reduced to fourteen. It remains for the zealous student to restore the ladder—to fill in some of the gaps between each step—as a result of his own earnest effort in discrimination.

*The Office of the Mighty Archangel of the Ray
of Orange is the Harmonizing of Will and Intellect.*

ORANGE RAY ATTRIBUTES

Anti-Gravitational LIGHT——Purity of High (GOD) Self

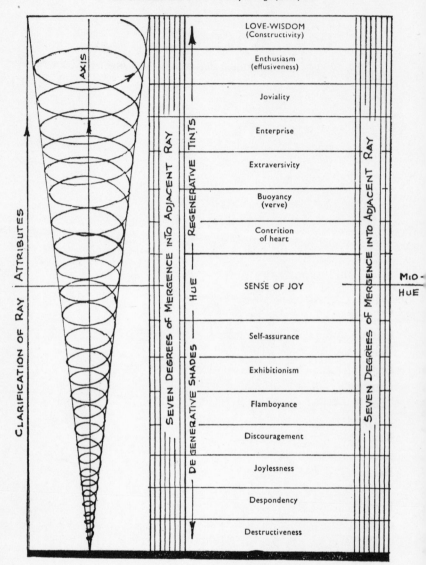

LOVE-WISDOM
(Constructivity)

Enthusiasm
(effusiveness)

Joviality

Enterprise

Extraversivity

Buoyancy
(verve)

Contrition
of heart

SENSE OF JOY

Self-assurance

Exhibitionism

Flamboyance

Discouragement

Joylessness

Despondency

Destructiveness

AXIS

CLARIFICATION OF RAY ATTRIBUTES

SEVEN DEGREES OF MERGENCE INTO ADJACENT RAY

REGENERATIVE TINTS

HUE

DEGENERATIVE SHADES

SEVEN DEGREES OF MERGENCE INTO ADJACENT RAY

MID-
HUE

Gravitational silt, precipitated by small-self

Chapter VI

ATTRIBUTES OF THE ORANGE RAY ANALYSED

"Bring now to bear—O Warrior of Light—
Fire of thy Love-Transmuted Will
To rouse thy Intellect from stup'rous sleep,
That from its unrefined latent Gold
Be burnt away incrusted dross of old.

A robe thus weave on loom of selfless Love—
Its warp, thy will, transmuted flame of Rose,
Its woof, transmuted intellect of Gold
To add its Joyous radiance of tone
Unto the Mighty 'Aum' around God's Throne."[1]

WHEN God's Creative Plan was made known to His Sons, "Cherubim and Seraphim went forth and sang for Joy". The Cherubim and Seraphim, the Mighty Archangels, are Those Who returned Home to The Father on the First Round out, resplendent in Their Robes of Light and Colour. They are the Directives of the Mind of God, and the Guardians of mankind. "For I shall give My Angels charge over thee."

The office of the Mighty Archangel of the vitalizing Orange Ray is the harmonizing of Will and Intellect in joyous constructivity. Orange symbolizes the union, or fusion, of The Father's *Will* (Red) with the Golden Intellect of the Mother of Wisdom. In Arcane records this Ray is often referred to as the Love-Wisdom Ray—Love being an aspect of Will. The song of this exalted union is one of Creative Joy.

The cellular reconstruction of man's coat of flesh—the anabolitic aspect of metabolism—is impelled by the constructive intent of *Atma*, reflected in the cell's centrosome,

[1] Ex Poem in a Master Monograph issued by *AMICA*, Temple of Radiance, Inc.

functioning through the frequencies of Orange. Orange works resurgently in all man's vehicles subtle and flesh.

On the level of Soul it fosters the budding and flowering of the Soul's Intent in incarnation, acting as a Golden Pollen. On the mental level its germinative sunshine impels 'seed ideas' to burst through the shell of their confinement. On emotional levels its motive power is emotive, raising the desire-element into higher registration of constructivity. Under the warming and encouraging impulses of Love-Wisdom man behaves much as a plant struggling from bondage of earth to release its flowering fragrance to the Sun.

Orange impels release from fixation and this liberation evokes Joy. As in the metallurgic furnace the refining flame burns away the dross and releases the pure metal, so likewise does the Orange flame operate in man.

In the Etheric Body which sustains the coat of flesh the refining Orange flame is seen raising Red in the Root Chakram. This Orange raised into the Splenic Chakram—the constructive-distributive centre—is seen flecked with every other colour of the rainbow, as a refiner of Ray Attributes. In this function Orange has complementation with Indigo.

Joy is the Mighty Magnet the burning zeal of which frees and refines the metals of Prodigals upon Earth, raising the atomic weight and thus speeding the Return Home. The Song of Orange is one of release and liberation from the bondage of self.

Children engaged in joyous play are unaware of themselves as creatures of Earth, nor are they aware of the outer-trappings and tribulations of the world around them. The fondly following eyes and yearning hearts of watching adults perceive this freedom and release and partake, momentarily, of this spirit of liberation—for Joy is unaware of self, time, or place.

An inventor immersed in constructive activity hears not the demands of the outer world—his consciousness is temporarily transported. Joy is at the heart of enthusiastic constructivity and it lifts ingenuity along on buoyant waves of assurance and certainty.

The word 'Enthusiasm' comes from the Greek—'en' meaning 'in' and the root 'theos' meaning 'God'. Thus 'Enthusiasm' really means to be infused with God. Zeal similarly relates to Zeus, and joviality to Jove. Thus were the Orange Ray Attributes anciently deified.

In the heart chakram petals of Golden Orange alternate with those of soft Green, serving to warm and enlighten the heart of man. Because the Joy of Orange frees one from consciousness of self (small-self) it impels extraversion as against introversion. By reason of its purifying warmth it produces the contrite heart—the heart touched by Love and Wisdom and awakening recognition of the Grace of God (Salmon-Pink). The tints of Orange are all regenerative to the heart, aid circulation, and exalt Will and Intellect.

If you do not find Orange in your character-analysis do no be dismayed. Possibly you have the clear Yellow of decisiveness and the bright Red of persistence which combine in a brotherhood of constructive Orange. There are characteristic affiliations in frequencies of Light as well as in shadow.

If in self-analysis is found lack of Orange there will undoubtedly be concommitant insufficiency of Joy, verve and buoyancy in one's behaviourism. The rust of frustration and the grey clouds of fear can be removed and dispelled by cultivation of the attributes of clear Orange. Enterprise is lifeless without the element of Joy. Plodding undertakings become all too grave without the anti-gravitational enthusiasm of Orange.

Maybe, in your honest analysis you have found a dark Red of obstinacy, and a debased Yellow of pessimism, together producing a dark brown of inaction. Liberation from both can be attained through introduction of clear Orange or by the cultivation of its attributes.

The shades of traits on differing Rays often combine in dark affiliation. For instance, Disbelief on the dark side of the Blue may combine with lack of Humour on the Green—both need a rising agent such as Orange. Thus we may use the tools of Light intelligently in effective remedial action.

Viewing the descending Scale of Orange Ray Attributes we see the ego motivated in self-will, and in pervert freedom of choice, lowering its consciousness in small-self gratifications. It seizes upon Orange to boost its self-esteem. The glowing power of Orange is perverted into exuberant self-assurance and flamboyant exhibitionism.

In ever deepening shades as Light departs from the heart, so departs the essence of Joy, and enterprise is deflated into discouragement. No longer on the crest of the wave the heart sinks into the shades of despondency—to the muddy bottom of the pond. In the chill of perverted Will and Intellect the stony heart turns to destructiveness, and instead of liberation it gathers the lethal shrouds of death.

The power of Orange can be likened to the office of the Commanding Officer of a regimental corp of army engineers. This service builds pontoons and bridges. It creates lines of communications, and builds operational units and bases. It performs reconstructional work and repairs. It constructs the facilities for the free function of the army in the field and zealously prepares the way for facile fulfilment of tactics and stratagems. It also does the demolition work of underground destruction. Similarly, in the Scale of Orange Ray Attributes we find Constructivity above, and destructivity below.

The higher attributes of Orange can be marshalled into the capsule of one cardinal quality to which has been given the name of Joy. The 'Y' symbolizes supplicant man with his arms uplifted in the contrition of his yearning heart. The 'J' represents the shepherd's crook with which, through constructive enterprise, man would gather his lambent potentials within his enfolding embrace. The 'O' indicates the fold of rounded-out completion over which the shepherd, his guardian High Self, lovingly hovers.

The family of man's potentialities gather around the hearth which is the heart of his home—where he seeks comfort, warmth and good cheer. At this centre of his life he finds courage and renewed enterprise to go forth, with the dawn of a new day, into the fields of enthusiastic constructivity.

SCALE OF INDIGO RAY ATTRIBUTES

Anti-Gravitational LIGHT——Purity of High (GOD) Self

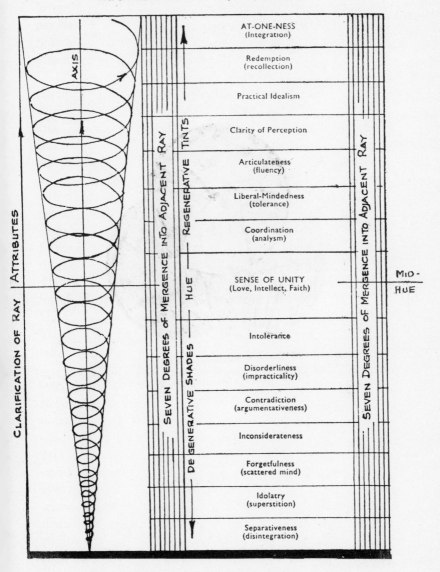

CLARIFICATION OF RAY ATTRIBUTES

AXIS

SEVEN DEGREES OF MERGENCE INTO ADJACENT RAY

REGENERATIVE TINTS

HUE

DEGENERATIVE SHADES

SEVEN DEGREES OF MERGENCE INTO ADJACENT RAY

MID-HUE

AT-ONE-NESS
(Integration)

Redemption
(recollection)

Practical Idealism

Clarity of Perception

Articulateness
(fluency)

Liberal-Mindedness
(tolerance)

Coordination
(analysm)

SENSE OF UNITY
(Love, Intellect, Faith)

Intolerance

Disorderliness
(impracticality)

Contradiction
(argumentativeness)

Inconsiderateness

Forgetfulness
(scattered mind)

Idolatry
(superstition)

Separativeness
(disintegration)

Gravitational silt, precipitated by small-self

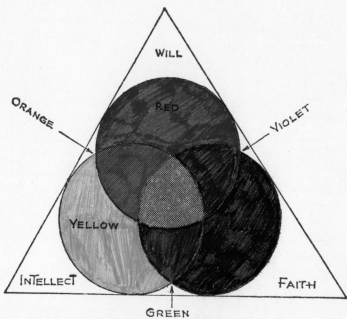

THE THREE PRIMARIES and THE FOUR SECONDARIES, Including INDIGO, the Unique
(because it embraces All and is the Threshold into the New)

Chapter VII

ATTRIBUTES OF THE GREEN RAY ANALYSED: THE IMPORTANCE OF BALANCE IN HUMAN CHARACTER

"... He maketh me to lie down in green pastures ... surely goodness and mercy shall follow me all the days of my life ..."

The 23rd Psalm

"The quality of mercy is not strained ..."

The Merchant of Venice

THE office of the Mighty Archangel presiding over the frequencies of consciousness registering as Green is the blending of Intellect with Soul Mind. Verily, many of the good things in life arrive through exercising the attributes of the Green Ray. They inflow and flourish in accord with the degree of balance brought into awareness. The Yellow of Intellect, in the Green Ray, is brought into the poise of control by the perceptual serenity of the Soul Mind.

The poise inwardly necessary to the practice of Yoga comes from the union of the frequencies of Yellow and Blue in Green. In poise there is passivity—truly, pass-ability. Only through this equipoise is channelship of Light possible. Only in this equilibrium can Light pass into our consciousness. Poise and control are synonymous.

Humility is an aspect of poise, and true humility arises from an inmost sense of justice—the result of unequivocal self-examination and the weighing of the findings in the scales of balance.

By no accident does the ancient symbol of the pair of scales hang above the entrance to Law Courts for the scales represent equity, and through equity to arrive at justice and judgment.

Judgment is not always the equivalent of justice in man's law. Real judgment is a Divine Prerogative—not a human. Justice to the Soul is arrived at upon the Scales of Karma, poised in perfect equity. But God ever extends the mercy of His Grace which pervades All Creation.

When we would treat another as we would ourselves an equitable balanced relationship is established and the qualities of sympathy and mercy are evoked for we are thus sharing an experience as a brother. In such relationship the quality of mercy is unlikely to be strained but extended toward generosity.

Sympathy (as with its higher consort, Compassion) is the handmaiden to understanding. For when we identify ourselves with another in the brotherhood of true sympathy there is friendly rapport—the quality evinced by the Good Samaritan.

Co-operation is the fruit of sympathy and friendship. Co-operation is impossible in unfriendly antipathy. Friendship embraces the wide-margined tolerance of agreement to disagree.

Out of the scales of friendship, as they tip up and down, we see ourselves through the eyes of another, we gain truer perspective—and this applies between nations as it does between individuals. As we see our reflection in the kindly mirror of friendship aspects of our behaviourism of which we have been unconscious are often suddenly highlighted to the extent that they seem laughably ridiculous. After the initial shock of disbelief the pendulum swings back to a point of truth and acceptance, and we are forced to laugh at ourselves. The ability to laugh at oneself is actually a refreshing experience, and it is a balancing factor. We arrive at a new centre of poise from which we can go forward.

Humour and laughter help to shake us free from the rigidity of fixations, making our attitudes more flexible and adaptable, making it possible to rise above situations of limitation. In true levity there is levitation, and liberation.

Of all nations renowned for humour the one nourished in the Emerald Isle has shown the greatest adaptability in fusion with other nations. At the same time it must be borne in mind that a perpetual sense of injustice can fall into the shadows of ingrained grievance—a lower aspect of the Green Ray consciousness.

The Jewish Race also portrays many of the characteristics of Green. The common-denominator between the Irish and the Jews preponderates in New York. This was exemplified in one of the most beloved of plays, *Abie's Irish Rose*, which holds the greatest long-run record because of the humorous truth it exuded.

The sense of justice fostered by the balance of Green is based in Conscientiousness—weighing in the scales of conscience. This introduces the attributive factor of 'critical discrimination'. Although there is the modern tendency to consider 'critical' and 'discrimination' with the adverse conjunctive of 'against' the qualifying adjective 'critical' really means 'in crisis' or 'impartial', taking neither part but weighed in the crux of balance.

Caution, one result of critical discrimination, is not necessarily a negative clamped-down attribute. There can be caution against uncharitableness. The real negative of generosity is miserliness. In the immortal psychological play, *The Merchant of Venice*, the quality of mercy was missing in the miser Shylock. The greatest misery a miser can experience is to find that which he cherishes finally valueless or impermanent.

Miserliness, non-sharing, is an adversary almost at the base of the scale of Green Ray propensities and is portrayed in the dark bottle-greens of self-confinement.

Precocity is a lack of self-control and humility. The precocious infant or individual may be exceeding bright in some respects but is imbalanced withal. Precocity is prematurity and immaturity.

Prejudice is pre-judgment and can be either for or against.

But it harbours darkness either way because prejudice judges prematurely before the true facts are known. It is disagreeable, disturbing, disqualifying. Its bias springs from emotionally-impelled thinking leading to distortion of evaluation. True evaluation evolves only in the balance of equity.

Suspicion, another dark Green adversary, is critical discrimination, or perspicacity, that has taken the wrong turning and gone underground to darkness. It undermines auspicious perspicacity.

Callousness is the opposite to sympathy—the hard shell of extreme indifference. A callus, which occurs usually on the feet, is a circumscribed hardening and thickening of the skin. In terms of colloquial understanding we term the callous person 'thick skinned'.

Indifference is one of the worst vices on the Green degenerative scale for it takes part in the one great heresy, that of Separateness. It begets the unhappy extremity of loneliness, lack of friendship, and isolation.

It will be seen from this analysis that all the Attributes of the Green Ray point to balance. Green is a great catalyst, the presence of which enables man's extremities to be harmonized and resolved, and the out-of-balance brought into rhythm.

No one can be in rhythm with the Universal flow of Energy without the balance of Green. For Prana flows through the poise of this balance.

Why is one not in balance? Because of the taking in more of one frequency than another. Too much of a good thing means starvation of another necessity. The body can dispense with what it does not need, but too much of one robs the individual of another.

Our misery can come from having too much of a commodity. This is miserliness and we thus deny ourselves other lighted currencies needed in circulation for our wealth of well-being.

The weighing in the scales of Green, attributively, helps

the body to balance its economy and to round out its fulfilment.

"Learn more and more to see through eyes of Soul" is an
injunction from on High. As the eyes of Soul (Blue) see more
and more through the eyes of Intellect (Gold) the balanced
view of Green becomes our verdant blessing.

The Office of the Mighty Archangel of the Indigo Ray is harmonization through the process of recapitulation of all the Rays.

The Office of the Mighty Archangel of the Ray of Green is the Blending of Intellect with Soul.

GREEN RAY ATTRIBUTES . . .
THE SCALES OF BALANCE AND JUSTICE

Anti-Gravitational LIGHT——Purity of High Self

BALANCE — POISE
(Control)

Justice
(True Humility)

Sympathy
(understanding)

Generosity-Humour
(sharing)

Cooperation
(adaptability)

Critical
discrimination

Conscientiousness
(caution)

SENSE OF EQUITY
(brotherliness)

Precocity

Prejudice
(disagreeableness)

Suspicion
(envy)

Lack of: judgment,
humour, humility

Callousness
(indifference)

Miserliness
(non-sharing)

Grievance (sense of
injustice)

SEVEN DEGREES OF MERGENCE INTO ADJACENT RAY

REGENERATIVE TINTS

HUE

DEGENERATIVE SHADES

SEVEN DEGREES OF MERGENCE INTO ADJACENT RAY

MID-HUE

INTELLECT
(YELLOW)

SOUL MIND
(BLUE)

Gravitational silt, precipitated by small-self

Chapter VIII

ATTRIBUTES OF THE INDIGO RAY ANALYSED; THE INDIGO THRESHOLD OF RECALL, AND OF CLARIFICATION

"From the hearts of the Seven Archangels of Heaven rose a Song of Praise unto God and His Son, The Word. Surged from Their hearts the Colours of The Seven Rays to swirl in ecstasy about the Throne of God. This was the first *Aum*, the Eternal Song of Love of God."[1]

The office of the Mighty Archangel of the Indigo Ray is harmonization, through the process of recapitulation, of all the Rays. In Indigo is the uniting of *Love-Will*, *Intellect* and *Soul Power—Red*, *Yellow* and *Blue*.

If we study the diagram on the opposite page we shall see how the three Secondaries of Orange, Green and Violet are formed from the three Primaries of *Red*, *Yellow* and *Blue*, with the fourth Secondary, Indigo, partaking of each at the centre.

Understanding of the power inhering in the Indigo Ray can best be gained in this graphical manner. These three circles, with the circumference of each circle touching the centre of each of the others, form a clover-leaf pattern. Colour each circle with one of the three primaries Red, Yellow, Blue. Where two adjacent colour circles overlap, in each instance, appear the three secondaries, Orange, Green, Violet. Where all three circles overlap at the core appears Indigo.

At this central core the three Primaries and the three Secondaries have a common-denominator where they are at-one, or integrated. We can now see the reasonableness of the Attributes of the Indigo Ray, and how they all fall into line as expressions, or exhibits, of a fundamental principle of Unity.

[1] Ex Monograph Instruction issued by *AMICA*, Temple of Radiance, Inc.

Man has seven sensory-motor association areas in the brain (five only given in textbooks of modern medical science). These are the brain areas of registration where senses are co-ordinated with the functional organs of the body, under the control of the thalamus. Each of these response areas is attuned to a different colour in the spectrum, and each has its own record of experience, with thalamic Indigo on the threshold the over-all keeper of the archives.

Since in the sensory spectrum Indigo is a combination, and co-ordinator, of the frequencies of the other six senses it has lines of communication comparable to telephone lines that operate in specialized frequencies. Thus, Indigo, at the thalamic switchboard, can tune-in to any of the other six sensory repositories and learn of its inventory.

This explains how Indigo has power of recall, or recollection, of the experiences of the Soul in its cyclic sojourns on Earth, and in other realms—in the frequencies of consciousness of the Red, Orange, Gold, Green, Blue, Indigo and Violet Rays. Through recall, with Indigo tapping the memory archives, an overall review and evaluation of experience becomes possible.

In recall is the power of redemption, for when we recollect we redeem.

It is said in Holy Writ that The Great Redeemer (Who functions in this capacity in the Indigo frequencies) redeems us through the forgiveness of sins (our toxic nature). In forgiveness we are freed from the hold of the sense of guilt—purged and purified. Redemption, purgation and purification thus go together.

In Arcane teaching the Indigo Ray is often referred to as the Indigo Cosmic Fire of purgation which cleanses the astral-emotional vehicles.

Another term of purification is clarification—to make clear the understanding. We use the term 'clarification' particularly in association with the mind, or the consciousness, i.e. in clarifying our concepts. And every silt-ladened cell is a unit of consciousness.

Only when the mind is clear and co-ordinated can we express ourselves adequately. Hence Indigo impels the attributes of expression, articulation, and co-ordination.

Recall, Redemption, Clarification are all regenerative attributes of the Indigo Ray operating towards the clear integration of consciousness.

Because Indigo is a common-denominator to the other six Rays the power of analysm is manifoldly manifested amongst its properties. The aphorism: 'To know all is to understand all; and to understand all is to forgive all' unfolds in the Indigo Ray Attributes of Liberality and Tolerance.

These Attributes were, and are, exemplified by The Great Redeemer Who, in His Indigo Ray Consciousness, is 'All things to All Men'.

Out of the practical attributes of all the Rays comes with Indigo a *fusion* of practicality. Applied perception of the high ideals summiting All Rays. Thus, Indigo is the Ray of Practical Idealism providing ample means for fulfilment.

In Arcane teaching the Indigo Ray is referred to as The Threshold. It is only through the power of recall that we can review past experiences, and by sifting these experiences glean the gold therein. As through clarification we shake ourselves free of accumulated dross we can step forward with our enduring treasure into the New. At the end of each cyclic round is the Indigo frequency of consciousness, the Threshold to a New Age.

Those who pass by, or decline to enter through, this summit Doorway descend again into the cyclic rounds of toils and trials to accept at some far-distant time again the opportunity on the Threshold. Meanwhile in the lower shades of Indigo propensities they seek their sheltered caves to indulge the luxury of Intolerance, the opposite to Liberality, the sloth of disorderliness that blights the bud of practicality.

As Light departs from its hue Indigo deepens towards pitch black, and in this descent comes the forgetfulness of the scattered mentality unable to recall, the inconsiderate view instead of the considered review, confusion instead of suffusion and infusion, idols replace ideals, separativeness and disintegration usurp the unity of integration. In deepest Indigo comes obsessive illusion, and the prize of the Soul itself is fought for in disillusion.

In these depths clear analysm gives way to contentious argumentation and many words slay *The Word*.

On the Indigo Ray are powerful attributes for regeneration in accord with the degree of White Light suffusing the tints. Equally powerful are the ominous shadowed propensities which together make a veritable toboggan for back-sliding downhill.

Indigo is the razor's edge. Under the searching Light of the Indigo Ray canopy man is face to face with himself, confronted by *All* that he is. Such is the Dweller on the Threshold.

Girded in Light of Resolution the Prodigal can face what he has made of himself throughout the aeons with his prerogative of freedom of choice. In the coalescence of countless experiences he can redeem his God-given Light and go forward with strengthened resolve into the New.

The word 'coalescence' can be considered to be a combination of 'coal' and 'essence'. The Dweller on the Threshold may be dark of face. But pitchy coal darkly glistens with all the colours of the Rainbow—all colours composing Indigo are there. And within is the Essence that can liberate the dark-held colours into Light.

Out of such a piece of coal, under pressure, can be produced the pure Diamond scintillating with flashing Colour at its heart. In this diamond we see the potentials of Indigo raised to the Heights. Such too is man who, passing over the Indigo Threshold, is raised to the White Light of The Christ Consciousness.

"Indigo is as the starry canopy of night, velvet and deep, graced with the Divine Effulgence of the White Christ Light. Lift High thy aspirations and find the Light of Truth within Indigo's multi-toned diamond depths."

SEVENTH . . .

Stood Fourth the Mighty Archangel of the Violet Ray, Whose Office is the Transmuting, following Recapitulation, of all the Rays.

SCALE OF VIOLET RAY ATTRIBUTES

Anti-Gravitational LIGHT——purity of High (GOD) Self

Gravitational silt, precipitate of small-self

ATTRIBUTES OF THE VIOLET RAY ANALYSED: THE CULMINATIVE RAY OF TRANSMUTATION AND TRANSLATION.

Arch Ray man-earthed to power, pomp, might—
Rich robed in Arrogance, made poor in plight,
With dominance demeaned by self-possessive 'right'
Transmute beneath Thy Dome, translate this blight!

Inheriting Son, with inner treasures bright,
To warm thy pledged Soul in heart contrite—
Keen intuition's fragrance, O full incite,
The flowering fullness Infinite!

THE Violet Ray is produced from the wedding of the Red of *Love-Will* and the Blue of *Soul Mind*. The phoenix-child of this union is re-birth of awareness of the Soul's Intent, sometimes spoken of as the 'twice-born'.

In the clarifying of recall in Indigo the Soul's purpose in incarnation has come to light—the purpose to which the Soul dedicated its Light upon setting out on its prodigal journey into the fields of experience and of service. In the Violet Ray frequency of consciousness the precious jewel of the Soul's Intent has been redeemed. In surrender of small-self Will, Soul impelled, this redeemed jewel of Intent is placed in reverent dedication as an offering upon the High Altar of the Sacred Inner Shrine within the Soul's heart, and joy gratitude for the revelation.

Impelled by the seraphic Blue of Soul Mind the wayward small-self ego long pervert now reverts, and in freedom of choice, places its petty will upon the Altar in service to

Almighty Will, in transmutation of desire. In sacrifice of small-self Will man re-dedicates himself to the advancing of his long-hidden Soul's Intent as an unique instrument of service to The Father.

Intuition is the bright star of alertness that scintillates in the crown-like firmament of his higher faculties. Its amethyst flash is the symbol of Ideals purified.

The High Desire of *Atma* in the Soul's heart is to redeem the Light of which it was once so prodigal in the kingdoms of its sojourn which finalized in flesh. In the fullness of sincere supplication in the Violet Ray consciousness the effulgence of the White Light of *Atma* is invoked. This God-given Light of *Atma*, drawing upon great reservoirs of Light infuses the Violet frequencies and raises the tone of every cell in man's vehicles both subtle and flesh, and establishes rapport between them.

Through this rapport man's garment of flesh is more greatly suffused by the Light of its Etheric Sustaining vehicle, which itself is violet in tone. This violet-toned Ether inducted into the bloodstream infuses every cell of the body which it feeds and purifies, and thus raises the cellular tone. This is transmutation of the coat of flesh.

All regenerative processes are anti-gravitational, whereas all degenerative processes are gravitational. Hence as the process of transmutation slowly continues the cells of the garment of flesh are less conditioned by the Law of Gravity. The moment arrives when in utter surrender to The Father's Will, and for the fulfilment of the Soul's Intent in service to The Father, the physical body can be transported and by-pass the grave. Now based in Anti-Gravitational Light, instead of based in gravitational darkness, the Soul infused garment can be raised or lowered in frequency for the purposes of the Soul's Intent—the Intent of *Atma* which is in complete accord with The Father's *Will*.

One of the facilities so dearly sought by man on this Violet Road is extra-sensory-perception. This additional sensory-perception is validly arrived at through Apperception.

Just as a mountain, or a sky-scraper, is built one level upon another, so Apperception is towered by one level of perception layered upon another—the perceptions of all the seven senses. The crowning story of the sky-scraper of Apperception—what might be called the penthouse—is created by Intuition, the highest faculty of Love-Will, Soul impelled.

Rabindranath Tagore, the great poet, artist, philosopher, mystic, has said: "The greatest work an artist can create is the artistry performed upon himself." When man has performed the highest Art upon himself all outer expressions of his Art are transformed and have a more powerful and compelling message to the beholder. The artist, then being in a higher state of realization, expresses of the nature of that realization.

The Sense of Power, and the use of Power, is in the balance-point of the Violet Ray. Whether it be applied 'upwards' in regeneration or 'downwards' in degeneration, depends upon the orientation of the particular Soul's motivation at its stage of involution-evolution, terrestrial-wards or Celestial-wards.

Purple is the robe of Kings, the symbol of the wielding of terrestrial power, the exhibition of superiority.

Portrayal of the perverted purple is evidenced in that characteristic of the superiority-complex we term 'snobbishness'—the result of over-weaning self-esteem.

Darker adversaries still are the mercenaries of Arrogance and Fanaticism, who wreak their own specialized havoc in the human kingdom. Amongst this clan are those who persist in monopolization of attention. They are never team-workers for they will rush out of their appointed position, seize and hold the ball and refuse to pass it to others. Of all fell traits 'treachery' on the deep dark Purple end of the Violet Ray is perhaps the worst traitor of all to the Soul.

Magicians, and sleight-of-hand artists, and illusionists, use the power of the Violet Ray to mislead and delude. Hypnotists use its power to intrude upon the domain that is rightly *Atma*'s. Whatever man's dilemma he can validly overcome and grow in strength only as he reaches up for the aid of *Atma*, his God-Self, whose All-Seeing Eye alone should direct him.

A lighter Violet Ray Attribute, but subject to shadow by ulterior motive, is the quality of Subtelty—sub-telepathy—undermining or over-shadowing that which is obvious. Subtelty perversely functions in subterfuge—such as the Trojan Horse to capture the citadel. It is a wonderful acquisition employed in altruistic use, and most dangerous when deployed in dark and devious intent.

Subtelty is an instrument of exceeding refinement impelled by Intuition. It can exalt Aspiration or exasperate to the point of expiration.

Belief is an attribute of Soul Power on the Blue Ray. When Belief is combined with the Red Ray attribute of Persistence the result is unshakeable Belief and One-Pointedness (Violet). Believe in the One Word. Many beliefs contend together and result in disbelief; many words slay *The Word*. When we get beyond words *Light* speaks; *Sound* speaks; *Fragrance* speaks—the language that is the product of the blending of Colour and Sound. All are universal and are expressive of *The One*.

The Soul on its prodigal journey started out in utter Simplicity (Innocence), and begat Complexity. In the Prodigal's return the Soul comes back, in inner-knowing-sense, to Simplicity (Wisdom).

It can be seen, by use of the Colour-Alphabet, that the word 'Wisdom' has an initial impact vibrating to Violet with Orange-Yellow (Gold) at its centre. There is a colour-correspondence here with the Wisdom Chakra at the top of the head—The Thousand-Petalled Lotus—the outer multi-toned petals of which are suffused with Violet, and the centre pure Gold, the Alpha and Omega.

Violet, being the colour of transmutation is symbolic of Eternal Life. But the dark side of the symbol is associated by man with Death. Both the light and the dark symbols are presented in the traditional draping of funeral coffins in Violet.

Every planet, as with individuals, at the end of a round or cycle, goes into the frequency of Violet after which it goes either down into the Astral shades or up into the Etheric Light —either to destruction, or to re-construction in the lift into a new round in the evolutionary spiral. Violet is always at the end of a cycle for the raising of tone into the New.

When a Soul comes to the end of a cycle of experience it is always on the Violet Ray. The individual by that time has accrued Power, but is he standing in Wisdom? Is he now going forward or turning backward? That is the question.

The Way of Transmutation is called the Royal Road—the Road of Power. The word 'Power' analysed on the Colour-Alphabet vibrates to Violet and Golden Yellow.

The Colour-Alphabet Key can be used in many ways which the student can learn for himself according to his prevailing interests. For instance, the initials to the names given nations and countries reveal their power, office of service, and their destiny.

The pineal and pituitary glands when violating in harmony produce together a transcendent Violet. These glands situated around the thalamus control the body's consciousness. The use of mantras, incenses and drugs excite these centres not necessarily in balance. Some of the drugs at the present time used to incite extra-sensory-perception actually neutralize and dull perception and bar the influx of Soul Light.

The Gates to the Kingdom cannot be forced. They are correctly entered by increase of transcendent Light in recognition of God's Grace. The only valid way to E-S-P is by transmutation of the individual's present perceptive attributes. If you have an attribute on the Violet Ray raise its tone by cultivating an affiliated attribute higher on the Ray Scale, thus introducing more White Light into your present Violet attribute and dissolving the gravitational sediment.

This is the manner in which the earnest progressive student uses the Ray Attribute Scales for Clarification. This is the valid evolutionary way and the Royal Road Home.

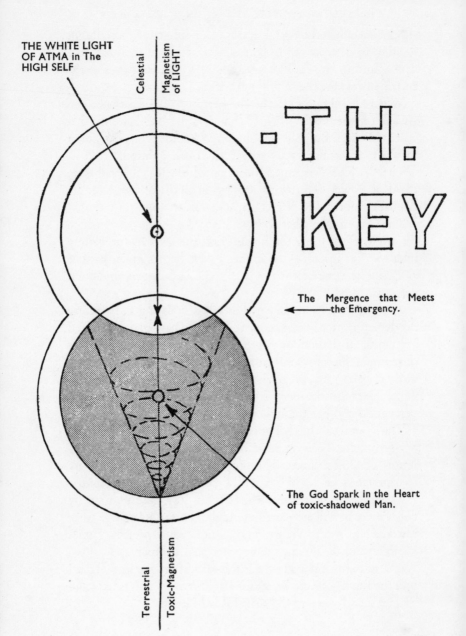

THE WHITE LIGHT OF ATMA in The HIGH SELF

Celestial

Magnetism of LIGHT

·TH.

KEY

The Mergence that Meets the Emergency.

The God Spark in the Heart of toxic-shadowed Man.

Terrestrial

Toxic-Magnetism

Chapter X

THE EIGHTH KEY EXPLAINED

THE figure 8 is formed of two circles linked, and upper and a lower. These two circles, one above the other, represent the ego functioning in the small, or low, self consciousness on Earth, and the Alter Ego, or High Self, abiding in the Heights —the God Self attuned to the Consciousness of The Father.

The lower circle thus symbolizes the prodigal son and the higher circle the Son who stayed at Home. Both are for ever linked in consciousness.

Man's destiny is to lift the consciousness of the lower into the higher so that his 8 becomes the O of completion. When man's Aspiration eclipses his Ambition the circles of his 8 are coincided. Then his stature is raised to full Height—his eight is aspirated.

To raise the consciousness of the gravitated, terrestrial, lower circle into the anti-gravitational, Celestial circle man has to remove the gravitational toxic silt by efforts in self-clarification. The primary purpose of the Scales of Ray Attributes given, and explained, in the foregoing chapters is to show the relationship existing between man's vices of darkness and his virtues of Light. The secondary purpose is to show that by dissolving the shadow in the vice the Life-Energy imprisoned therein may be released into the Light of its counterpart virtue. (Again vices and virtues are symbolized by the lower and higher circles of the 8.) This is transmutation.

The remaining step is to show *How* the dissolving of toxic shadow can be effected by techniques in Clarification which foster the fulfilment of the Soul's Intent. These are the steps upon man's own Jacob's Ladder which lead him from earthbound consciousness to the Heights. When the weight from his eight[1] is lifted he can rise to his Height. It will be noted that 'H' vibrates to Indigo which is the colour and Ray of Clarification.

At the centre of man's bodily universe—the physical body and its intermeshing subtler vehicles—is the Divine Spark within the Soul's heart. This Spark of Divine Intelligence ever wishes to produce the optimum in its bodily universe. The fulfilment of its Plan is thwarted by man's perverse self-will.

At the centre of man's Celestial Universe is *Atma* of the High Self (or Soul Twin) forever linked with the Atmic Spark of the prodigal Soul twin on Earth. This connection is an infinitely tenuous umbilical cord of Light, originating in, and coming from, *The Father-Mother God*. This beam of Light is directed through *Atma* in the Soul Twin in the Heights to the Atmic Spark circumscribed in the twin on Earth.

The perverse ingrained traits of man's character have throttled inflow of this *Light-Life-Energy* to his bodily universe. Instead of ease in influx has come the dis-ease of restriction. Starved of vigorous circulation silt has precipitated and crystallized.

To clear this *Life-Energy* channel man must change his direction from perversity to university. His character *crystallization* must be clarified, and his body freed, by character *Christalization*. Instead of his Life-view blinkered in small intents it must be expanded and raised to perceive the Grand Intent. He must ask of his High (God) Self that each day he sees, more and more, through eyes of Soul in every situation confronting him in relation to his fellowman, "having eyes too pure to behold iniquity (inequity)". And "when thine eyes (physical and Soul) are single thy whole body shall be full of Light".

To receive the Clarifying Light of The Father's Love through the Gate of *Atma* man must earnestly *Ask* for its

---

[1] The Figure '8' also symbolizes man's Karma which can be resolved in one lifetime, sometimes less, in complete realization of the Cardinal *Love-Will* Principle.

influx to dissolve the sedimented damming of the *Life-Stream*, which damming has been the long durance of his damnation. He must ardently pray for this restoration. As he prays his gates of praise will open and in the Grand Attitude he will be filled with Gratitude. This spirit of thankfulness should be as a fundamental stream flowing beneath the surface of one's daily routines constantly suffusing and refreshing one's attitudes.

Inflow of the Stream of Light through *Atma*, The God Spark, should be fostered by the following affirmation formula: "O *Mighty Atma, God within me, send through me, as Soul, thy healing ray!*"

This is the formula for induction of Light for the clarification of oneself and others.

Man's mentality has been so long conditioned by conflicting thoughts and desires that even the earnest beseechings rising from his yearning heart are wont to stray away from focused intent in meditation and prayer. To keep attention focused his affirmation should be confirmed in action.

Man's hands are the servers of his bodily realm. In each palm is a nerve plexus, the counterpart of a chakra of Light in the Etheric Sustaining Body. Man, as supplicant for himself and others, should inwardly ask that the Light of *Atma*, fed by The Father, shining through his Soul's heart, flow freely through the chakras in the palms of his two hands, upraised for use.[1]

Then, with the hands and fingers held loosely and flexibly about nine inches away from the physical body, and palms facing it, he should begin to beam this Soul Light of *Atma* over his entire body, starting from above the head. At this stage both hands hover together over the crown of the head as he holds his affirmative thought.

Joyous gratitude at the centre of his affirmative thought will act as a mighty magnet to *The Light of the Father's Love* flowing

[1] Ex Monographs on *The Light of the Father's Love*, issued by *AMICA*, Temple of Radiance, Inc., P.O. Box 173, Santa Barbara, Calif.

through his beloved Son, *Atma*, to sustain and clarify his garments subtle and flesh that the son has taken upon himself.

In beaming the Light of *Atma* upon the crown of the head man's pineal centre is progressively clarified, and his sense of intuition alerted.

Then the hands part and move down slightly, one over the brow and the other juxtapositioned at the back of the head so that the Light is beamed through from palm to palm and the pituitary-thalamic centres, and the allied senses of vision and balance, respectively, benefited.

The hands then move around to the ears, beaming the Light from the pole in one hand to the pole in the other, to clarify hearing. Subsequently the hands move down to hover over the carotid plexuses at the sides of the neck and the Light is beamed through to the laryngeal and pharyngeal areas which govern articulate speech.

Every organic area of the body, and its sensory-motor nerve centre, is beamed with *The Light of the Father's Love* through His representative, *Atma*, the Divine Spark.

This Radiance from *The Father* is *Love-Light-Life*. It is *Life-Energy* itself. How is this *Light* used for the purpose of the body's clarification and requirements? The Etheric prototype of every organic area, under the direction of *Atma*, takes from the White Light the Indigo frequency of Clarification and also selects the specific frequency of Colour needed for its restoration.[1]

This first frequency taken from the White Light, the Indigo Light of Clarification, because of its purifying potency is sometimes called the Indigo Cosmic Fire because it is a burning Light which consumes the precipitates of dross and debris in the cellular structure of the garment of flesh. The greater the clarification the greater the restoration.

As the *Light of Life* increasingly replaces the darkness of

[1] If beaming the Light of *ATMA* upon the torso of a friend wearing white clothing the colour changes can be seen projected on the white garment as the hands hover over different areas.

death in the cells of the garment of flesh the tone of the body is raised in frequency little by little. The Indigo Light of Clarification is the path-clearer for the influx of the Violet Light of Transmutation. When the Violet Light of trans-mutation pervades the cells, the metabolic processes causing change in the garment of flesh, come under its superior control. Anti-gravitational Light has victored over the adversary of gravitational darkness, and the grave is by-passed.

It should be borne fundamentally in mind that the pre-cipitates of silt in the garment of flesh have been caused by the perpetuation of character faults and habits. These long-held, and often cherished, faults in habits and attitudes have pro-duced precipitates that have combined and consolidated into a coagulum of tenacious gravitational glue. To practise with the Light of Clarification and to perpetuate a character fault is a contradiction to the Law involved. Practice of Clarification and of character correction must go hand in hand.

The purpose of this book with its explanation of the Colour-Key, and the Scales of Ray Attributes, is to aid this cooperative alignment.

This is an over-all explanation of the fundamental techniques in Light available to man when, having calmly reviewed the analysis of his character, its traits good and bad, he yearns actively to take part in, and to speed, his redemption.

Having weighed himself on the Scales, and continuing in practices of Clarification and restoration, the vice-virtue balance of his character alters. Aligned with his Soul's Intent the consciousness of man ascends the Ladder of Light and raises its garment of flesh with it.

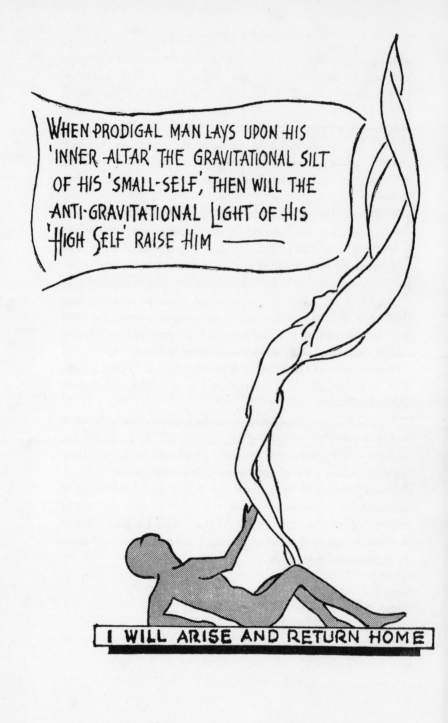

Chapter XI

THE OVER-ALL PLAN, AND THE INDIVIDUAL'S MOST VITAL PART THEREIN

IN this concluding chapter the effort is made to fulfil the need, to gather into one embrace towards their resolution in use, the Colour Key, the Scales of Ray Attributes, and the techniques in Light for character clarification and correction.

Indelibly to leave a compelling picture of the vital part the individual can, and eventually *must*, play in the Over-all Plan, the recapitulative words of the Mentor Spokesman for The High Arc of Light, in charge of this facet of instruction are directly quoted.

"Ye were, in the Beginning, At-One with God. Ye were One and indivisible from His Holy Body.

"Our Almighty Father, God, did will that He express Himself as individuated portions of Himself. He issued forth from Himself, Emanations of His Holy Being. These Emanations are His sons, compressed Seeds of Light.

"God sent forth His Seeds into the Fields of Experience, that they might gain knowledge, strength, wisdom, love and Light. In order that this be accomplished, His sons are required to grow and mature into state of reliability—of consciousness —as individual beings. In this manner does Our Father express Himself through His sons.

"A slight imbalance did God instigate in order to effect the necessary separation of His Emanations from Himself for this procedure. The separation is but *seeming* separation, for each Emanation (son) is eternally linked with his Father through a filament of Light which we call the Divine Umbilical cord.

"This slight imbalance which caused the issuing forth of God's Emanations is the process of Involution.

"In the beginning, the in-coiling was slight. Hence the circle of involution was vast, indeed. But as the spiralling inward continued, the circle contracted—grew smaller and smaller in area. The sons became more and more separated from their Source. During this increasing separation memories of their Father and their Homeland grew dim. This was in God's Will and Wisdom; for in His Great Plan each son must have his schooling, gain strength and wisdom, through his own efforts and experience.

"In the increasing separation of the sons of God from their Source, a certain cloud, or shadow, developed around the Seed of Light. And so the Seed of Light envestured himself with the various sheaths or vehicles, Soul, Spirit, Recorder, Etheric and flesh—that he might have experience on the various planes of consciousness, the intervening cloud, or shadow, between each vehicle increased in density forming an insulation.

"All creations not of God are not of Truth. All that is not Truth is illusion and delusion. Therefore the creations of God's sons in the fields of experience manifested, less and less, of their original perfection, less and less of God and Truth, as they continued in their journey away from Home. This is allowed by The Father in His Wisdom, for it constitutes the necessary schooling of His sons.

"The shadow or cloud we speak of, ye may comprehend, is the result of darkness—lack of Light—and thus of low and slow frequency, less tenuous and less expansive; and this in direct ratio to lack of Light. Therefore, as the sons of God moved in the spiral of involution *away* from Light the creations became more dense, material, gross, until the lowest point allowable was reached—the plane of Earth."

This was the state of hobbled man at the nadir, or aphelion—the farthest point out.

"The process of Evolution is the journey Home. As involution means becoming in-volved, coiling-in upon itself—becoming thus separated from Truth with the resulting complexities, perplexities and innumerable illusions and delusions—the process of Evolution means an exact reversal of this.

"It means the *reversal* of the process of involution. It means the uncoiling, in the opposite direction, of the Spiral of involvement. It means *extraction* from the perplexities, entanglements and confusions. It means the dispersal of the shadow of darkness which caused this condition. Therefore it means the return to Light, by the processes of Clarification, purification and purging.

"This will result in synchronizing and harmonizing with the Immutable law of God instead of travelling in the opposite direction—of opposing—the Law and will of God.

"No son of God is held accountable for his creations during the Involutionary Journey into the Fields of Experience; for in this process his memory was dimmed by Will of God, that he might learn from the resulting experiences. Our Father is ever wise, loving and just.

"But upon the Evolutionary Journey, the son is beginning to awaken from his dream of illusion, and to have memory restored to him. He is becoming cognizant again, of Light. Thus he is now held accountable for his creations, in direct ratio to his state, or level, of comprehension and awakening."

This is man's present state of crisis. He is swayed by the emotional opposites of low and High desires on the one hand, and by the conflict of mentalization in self-interest and Pure Intellect on the other. This is the cause of man's emotional-mental wobble.

"At intervals, God, The Divine Magnet, doth send forth *His Call* to His sons, bidding them return to Him. Man names these intervals 'cycles' or 'ages'. When three cycles or ages occur simultaneously, as in the present time, this is named a 'Major Cycle'. Major Cycles are rare, comparatively speaking, as to 'time', but this is in reality a state of progression of consciousness. In a Major Cycle such as man and his planet, Earth, now enter, God's Call is accompanied by a greater influx of *Light*. For *God Is Light*.

"*The Light of the Father's Love is His Call.* This Light, pervading the Cosmic Ray, is a frequency of Light that disperses all shadow, cloud and darkness—and hence, illusion.

"As we have said, and now, for thy clarity of comprehension reiterate, the shadow is first dispersed between the higher-frequency vehicles—the Seed of Light and its Soul and Spirit sheathes. Man has at present no direct conscious participation in this.

"But when the clarifying process extends to the Etheric, physical and astral planes of consciousness, man is required to play his part. This is because he is awakening to Light and Truth. He is upon the Homeward Journey.

"What man created during his journey downward in frequency, he is required now to disperse, and replace, with truer and ever truer manifestations of his awakening consciousness. He will gradually replace delusion and monstrous creations with those of increasing beauty, constructiveness and Light. And this will prevail until the son of God is Home—which means the final dispersal of *all* illusion.

"The greatest delusion in all Infinity is that of the small-self—the petty ego—the false personality of man. The small-self is frequently alluded to by those of Wisdom on the Higher Planes, as well as upon Earth, as the 'bottomless pit'. And the realm of consciousness inhabited by the small-self is often referred to as 'outer darkness'.

"In the delusions of small-self abide the seeds of 'death'—a creation of the small-self. It is created of the low frequencies aligned to the pull of Earth gravity—the pull of the grave. The final delusion to be overcome is 'death'. And since 'death' is a creation of the small-self, when the small-self is vanquished and dispersed, then will its foulest creation be no more.

"When the small-self, the 'dragon' which drags man on into the grave of its own delusions, is seen for what it is—but phantom—it will not be too difficult to dispense with.

"But we would have ye leave the transient, changing scene, to contemplate, with nobility of concept, the eternal verities.

"Think of the infinite beauties and wonders that await ye as Souls. Think *as* Soul of the eternal son of God nesting within thy heart—the Divine Seed of Light—glorious and powerful with the power and glory of thy Father, God.

"Dwell in reverent thought upon this, thanking thy Father for this very part of Him, linked eternally with Him through Love, inconceivable to thy human thinking, but not to thy deep response as Soul. Dwell in joyous anticipation, of all that lies ahead of ye on thy Homeward Journey to Him.

"Dwell in joyous anticipation of new vistas of unfoldment of achievement, of service, of ever-increasing love and wisdom —all awaiting thy quickening response, that ye may receive. Feel within thy being the surge of wonder arising from thy contemplation of the multitudinous spheres of ever-expanding consciousness yet to be traversed—with loving companions new-met, and those who in eagerness untold await reunion with ye. Yea, all Infinity with its boundless beauty, and Love unspeakable awaits ye.

"New tasks, new lessons, more illumined responsibilities, more worthy service—all far beyond thy present scope of comprehension, await thy feet upon the Path. Yea, treasures and glories laid up for ye before the foundation of this small Earth, will surely be thine.

"And all this in exchange for one small gift from thee—the gift to thy Father, God, of thy small-self will—the shadowy insubstantial illusion of thy small-self will. Illusion, in all Truth, it is. For it be but the creation of man's lowest pitch.

"Freedom of choice be thine: whether to cling yet longer to thy shadowy shrouds—thy winding cloths of involvement —or to rend them asunder and step forth—free for ever more. Strip away thy grave clothes and stand forth to thy full stature as free Soul, claiming thy Divine Heritage as son of God: Life-Eternal.

"We have limned but a faint sketch of that for which ye may be grateful. If for a few moments each day ye could, in un-clouded mind, dwell thus in thy thinking, from out thy

Sacred Inner Shrine would Light shine forth, to lift and strengthen all thy brothers upon the Way.

"A service such as this, rendered in joyous, silent humility and long gratitude, would help to light the world. It would start a blaze of response in Souls that would shake the Earth itself of dross and shadow. The extent of this, if ye could but

---

THIS CHRISTMAS TIDE

UNTO THY FATHER GOD, O MAN, BRING THEE THIS TIDE, A GIFT— THE ONLY GIFT THAT MAN CAN EVER GIVE TO HIM.

IT IS THINE OWN SMALL-SELF.

YEA, LAY UPON HIS ALTAR IN THY HEART, ALL OF THINE OWN SMALL-SELF—ITS WILL! ITS SMALL DESIRES! ITS ILLUSIONS AND ITS STRIFE.

"A GIFT?" YOU SAY—"A GIFT OF CONFLICT AND OF WOE— TO PLACE UPON THE ALTAR OF MY GOD?"

AH YES, BELOVED, 'TIS ALL THAT THOU DOST HAVE—UNTIL SURRENDERED FULL, IN JOYOUS TRUST, IN HEART CONTRITE AND BOWED.

A PRECIOUS THING HAST THIS ILLUSION BEEN TO THEE, AND THOU HAST HELD IT TIGHTLY TO THY HEART.

BUT NOW A CALL HAS WINGED TO THEE FROM OUT THE HEIGHTS— "BELOVED SON, STEP FORTH FROM OUT THY PRISON WALLS— THY EGO-BARS NOW REND ASUNDER. COME TO ME.

"THE DOOR OF THY DANK PRISON HOUSE HAS STOOD AJAR. FOR MANY AEONS HAS IT BEEN BUT VEIL—A DREAM OF THINE OWN FASHIONING.

see, would cause ye such depth of gratitude that ye, thyselves, would be lifted on waves of Light into higher spheres of consciousness.

"Dwell now upon this for we would have ye put it into practice. Join with us in this Lifting Frequency."[1]

[1] Ex The Master Monographs issued by *AMICA*, Temple of Radiance, Inc. P.O. Box 173, Santa Barbara California, U.S.A.

—THY GIFT

"NOW ON MY ALTAR LAY THY BURDEN DOWN. A HEAVY LOAD IT IS UPON THE SOUL. ALL SORROW, CONFLICT, LUST AND PASSIONS OF THE SELF ABIDE THEREIN—AND I, THY FATHER! GOD, WOULD HAVE THEE FREE.

"THE CHOICE, BELOVED, IS THINE OWN TO MAKE. AND WHEN THIS SELF IS FULL-SURRENDERED UNTO ME, I CROWN THEE BRIGHT, WITH A NEW DIADEM—THE DIADEM OF LIFE AND LOVE AND JOY."

O MAN, IN SPIRIT OF NOBILITY AND TRUST, UPON HIS HOLY ALTAR PLACE THY ALL.

AND WHEN AWAKENED FROM THY DREAM OF SELF, BENEATH THE LIGHT OF LOVE THAT IN THEE GLOWS, THEN WILT THOU SEE A TRUTH SUBLIME—

THE GIFT THOU HAST IN FULL SURRENDER MADE TO GOD, HAS BEEN A GIFT TO THINE OWN SOUL—TO THEE.

FOR AS A SON OF GOD AND HEIR OF HIM, ALL THAT HE HAS IS THINE. ALL THAT HE IS—IS THEE!

Selah,
Menelley